87 Low Cholesterol Recipes for Home

By: Kelly Johnson

Table of Contents

- Grilled Lemon Herb Chicken
- Quinoa Salad
- Baked Salmon with Dill
- Vegetable Stir-Fry
- Mango Salsa Chicken
- Egg White Omelette
- Sweet Potato and Black Bean Chili
- Shrimp and Avocado Salad
- Roasted Brussels Sprouts
- Lentil Soup
- Cauliflower Rice Stir-Fry
- Greek Salad
- Turkey and Veggie Skewers
- Baked Cod with Herbs
- Spinach and Feta Stuffed Chicken Breast
- Mushroom and Spinach Quiche (with Egg Whites)
- Cucumber and Tomato Salad
- Oven-Baked Turkey Meatballs
- Broccoli and Cheddar Stuffed Potatoes
- Sesame Ginger Tofu Stir-Fry
- Chickpea Salad
- Baked Chicken with Rosemary
- Zucchini Noodles with Pesto
- Salmon and Asparagus Foil Packets
- Tomato Basil Soup
- Asian-Inspired Cabbage Rolls
- Mango Avocado Quinoa Bowl
- Herb-Roasted Vegetables
- Stuffed Bell Peppers with Turkey and Brown Rice
- Garlic and Lemon Shrimp Skewers
- Pesto Zoodles with Cherry Tomatoes
- Cauliflower and Broccoli Soup
- Lemon Garlic Roasted Chicken
- Cucumber Roll-Ups with Hummus
- Black Bean and Corn Salad
- Balsamic Glazed Brussels Sprouts

- Tomato Basil Quinoa Stuffed Peppers
- Greek Yogurt Parfait with Berries
- Turkey and Vegetable Skillet
- Roasted Eggplant Dip (Baba Ganoush)
- Cilantro Lime Shrimp Lettuce Wraps
- Spaghetti Squash with Tomato Sauce
- Mushroom and Spinach Stuffed Chicken Breast
- Sweet Potato and Kale Hash
- Tuna and White Bean Salad
- Cabbage and Apple Slaw
- Grilled Veggie and Hummus Wrap
- Sesame Soy Marinated Tofu
- Mediterranean Quinoa Bowl
- Stir-Fried Brown Rice with Vegetables
- Lemon Herb Tilapia
- Cauliflower Mashed Potatoes
- Bruschetta Chicken
- Kale and White Bean Soup
- Avocado and Chickpea Salad
- Salmon and Quinoa Patties
- Broccoli and Cauliflower Gratin
- Spicy Grilled Shrimp
- Caprese Salad
- Chia Seed Pudding with Berries
- Sesame Ginger Chicken Stir-Fry
- Quinoa-Stuffed Bell Peppers
- Eggplant and Tomato Bake
- Roasted Red Pepper Hummus
- Lemon Herb Roasted Vegetables
- Miso Glazed Cod
- Stuffed Portobello Mushrooms
- Cucumber Avocado Soup
- Cilantro Lime Rice with Black BBeans
- Baked Chicken with Mustard and Herbs
- Mango Basil Chicken Lettuce Wraps
- Spaghetti Squash Primavera
- Cumin-Spiced Lentils
- Herb-Roasted Turkey Breast
- Ratatouille
- Turkey and Vegetable Kabobs

- Stuffed Acorn Squash
- Garlic Lemon Shrimp with Quinoa
- Cabbage and Carrot Slaw
- Mushroom and Spinach Stuffed Portobello Mushrooms
- Baked Cod with Mango Salsa
- Sweet Potato and Kale Frittata
- Tomato and Basil Stuffed Chicken Breast
- Cauliflower and Chickpea Curry
- Sautéed Spinach with Garlic
- Baked Teriyaki Salmon
- Pineapple and Black Bean Quinoa Bowl

Grilled Lemon Herb Chicken

Ingredients:

- 4 boneless, skinless chicken breasts
- 2 lemons (juiced)
- 3 tablespoons olive oil
- 3 cloves garlic (minced)
- 1 teaspoon dried oregano
- 1 teaspoon dried thyme
- 1 teaspoon dried rosemary
- Salt and pepper to taste

Instructions:

In a bowl, whisk together the lemon juice, olive oil, minced garlic, dried oregano, dried thyme, dried rosemary, salt, and pepper. This will be your marinade.

Place the chicken breasts in a large resealable plastic bag or shallow dish.

Pour the marinade over the chicken, making sure each piece is well-coated. Seal the bag or cover the dish and refrigerate for at least 30 minutes to allow the flavors to meld.

Preheat your grill to medium-high heat.

Remove the chicken from the marinade and let any excess drip off.

Grill the chicken breasts for about 6-8 minutes per side or until they are cooked through and have beautiful grill marks. The internal temperature should reach 165°F (74°C).

While grilling, you can baste the chicken with some of the remaining marinade to keep it moist and enhance the flavor.

Once the chicken is done, remove it from the grill and let it rest for a few minutes before serving.

Garnish with fresh herbs or additional lemon slices if desired.

Serve your Grilled Lemon Herb Chicken with your favorite side dishes like roasted vegetables, rice, or a fresh salad. Enjoy your delicious and healthy meal!

Quinoa Salad

Ingredients:

- 1 cup quinoa, rinsed
- 2 cups water or vegetable broth
- 1 cucumber, diced
- 1 bell pepper (any color), diced
- 1 cup cherry tomatoes, halved
- 1/2 cup red onion, finely chopped
- 1/4 cup fresh parsley, chopped
- 1/4 cup fresh cilantro, chopped (optional)
- 1/3 cup feta cheese, crumbled (optional)
- 1/4 cup extra-virgin olive oil
- 2 tablespoons lemon juice
- 1 teaspoon Dijon mustard
- Salt and pepper to taste

Instructions:

Rinse the quinoa thoroughly under cold water.
In a medium saucepan, combine the quinoa and water or vegetable broth. Bring to a boil, then reduce heat to low, cover, and simmer for about 15 minutes or until the quinoa is cooked and the liquid is absorbed.
Fluff the quinoa with a fork and let it cool to room temperature.
In a large bowl, combine the cooled quinoa, diced cucumber, bell pepper, cherry tomatoes, red onion, parsley, and cilantro.
In a small bowl, whisk together the olive oil, lemon juice, Dijon mustard, salt, and pepper to create the dressing.
Pour the dressing over the quinoa mixture and toss everything together until well combined.
If using, sprinkle the crumbled feta cheese over the salad and gently toss again.
Refrigerate the quinoa salad for at least 30 minutes before serving to allow the flavors to meld.
Adjust salt and pepper to taste before serving.

This quinoa salad is not only delicious but also packed with protein and nutrients. Feel free to add other vegetables, nuts, or seeds to suit your taste preferences. Enjoy your wholesome and flavorful quinoa salad!

Baked Salmon with Dill
Ingredients:

4 salmon fillets
2 tablespoons olive oil
2 tablespoons fresh dill, chopped
2 cloves garlic, minced
1 lemon, thinly sliced
Salt and pepper to taste
Lemon wedges for serving (optional)
Instructions:

Preheat your oven to 375°F (190°C).

Place the salmon fillets on a baking sheet lined with parchment paper or lightly greased.

In a small bowl, mix together the olive oil, chopped dill, minced garlic, salt, and pepper.

Brush the dill and garlic mixture evenly over each salmon fillet.

Place a couple of lemon slices on top of each fillet.

Bake in the preheated oven for about 15-20 minutes or until the salmon is cooked through and flakes easily with a fork. The cooking time may vary depending on the thickness of the fillets.

Once baked, remove the salmon from the oven and let it rest for a few minutes.

Serve the baked salmon with additional lemon wedges if desired.

This baked salmon with dill is not only a healthy option but also bursting with fresh flavors. You can pair it with a side of steamed vegetables, a salad, or your favorite grains for a well-balanced meal. Enjoy your delicious and nutritious dish!

Vegetable Stir-Fry

Ingredients:

- 2 tablespoons vegetable oil (such as sesame oil or peanut oil)
- 1 onion, thinly sliced
- 2 cloves garlic, minced
- 1-inch piece of ginger, grated
- 1 bell pepper, thinly sliced
- 1 carrot, julienned
- 1 zucchini, sliced
- 1 cup broccoli florets
- 1 cup snap peas, ends trimmed
- 1 cup mushrooms, sliced
- 1 cup baby corn, halved
- 2 tablespoons soy sauce
- 1 tablespoon oyster sauce (optional)
- 1 teaspoon sesame oil
- 1 tablespoon cornstarch mixed with 2 tablespoons water (optional, for thickening)
- Salt and pepper to taste
- Cooked rice or noodles for serving

Instructions:

Heat the vegetable oil in a wok or large skillet over medium-high heat.
Add the sliced onion, minced garlic, and grated ginger. Stir-fry for about 1-2 minutes until fragrant.
Add the bell pepper, carrot, zucchini, broccoli, snap peas, mushrooms, and baby corn to the wok. Stir-fry for 4-5 minutes or until the vegetables are crisp-tender.
In a small bowl, mix together the soy sauce, oyster sauce (if using), and sesame oil.
Pour the sauce over the vegetables and toss to coat evenly. Cook for an additional 2-3 minutes.
If you prefer a thicker sauce, add the cornstarch mixture to the stir-fry and cook until the sauce thickens.
Season with salt and pepper to taste.
Serve the vegetable stir-fry over cooked rice or noodles.

Feel free to customize this recipe by adding your favorite vegetables or protein sources like tofu, chicken, or shrimp. Vegetable stir-fry is a versatile and healthy option that can be adapted to suit your taste preferences. Enjoy your vibrant and flavorful stir-fried vegetables!

Mango Salsa Chicken

Ingredients:

For the Chicken:

- 4 boneless, skinless chicken breasts
- 2 tablespoons olive oil
- 1 teaspoon ground cumin
- 1 teaspoon smoked paprika
- Salt and pepper to taste

For the Mango Salsa:

- 2 ripe mangoes, peeled, pitted, and diced
- 1/2 red onion, finely chopped
- 1 red bell pepper, diced
- 1 jalapeño, seeds removed and finely chopped (optional for heat)
- 1/4 cup fresh cilantro, chopped
- Juice of 1 lime
- Salt and pepper to taste

Instructions:

Preheat your grill or grill pan to medium-high heat.
In a bowl, mix together the olive oil, ground cumin, smoked paprika, salt, and pepper. Coat the chicken breasts with this spice mixture.
Grill the chicken breasts for about 6-8 minutes per side or until they are cooked through and have nice grill marks. Make sure the internal temperature reaches 165°F (74°C).
While the chicken is grilling, prepare the mango salsa. In a separate bowl, combine diced mangoes, red onion, red bell pepper, jalapeño (if using), cilantro, lime juice, salt, and pepper. Mix well.
Once the chicken is done, remove it from the grill and let it rest for a few minutes.
Serve the grilled chicken with a generous spoonful of mango salsa on top.
Garnish with additional cilantro and lime wedges if desired.

This Mango Salsa Chicken is a perfect blend of flavors and textures, making it a great choice for a light and summery meal. You can serve it with rice, quinoa, or a side of mixed greens. Enjoy the burst of tropical goodness!

Egg White Omelette

Ingredients:

- 4 large egg whites
- 1 tablespoon olive oil or cooking spray
- Salt and pepper to taste
- 1/2 cup diced vegetables (e.g., bell peppers, onions, tomatoes, spinach)
- 2 tablespoons diced ham or cooked turkey (optional)
- 1/4 cup shredded cheese (optional)
- Fresh herbs (e.g., parsley, chives) for garnish

Instructions:

Separate Egg Whites: Crack the eggs and separate the egg whites from the yolks. You can save the yolks for another recipe.

Whisk Egg Whites: In a bowl, whisk the egg whites until frothy. Season with salt and pepper.

Preheat Pan: Heat the olive oil or coat a non-stick skillet with cooking spray over medium heat.

Sauté Vegetables: Add the diced vegetables to the pan and sauté for 2-3 minutes until they are softened.

Add Egg Whites: Pour the whisked egg whites over the sautéed vegetables. Allow them to set slightly around the edges.

Optional Additions: Sprinkle diced ham or cooked turkey over one half of the omelette. Add shredded cheese if desired.

Fold and Cook: Once the edges are set, carefully fold the omelette in half using a spatula. Cook for an additional 1-2 minutes until the egg whites are fully cooked.

Garnish and Serve: Slide the omelette onto a plate, garnish with fresh herbs, and serve hot.

Feel free to experiment with different vegetable combinations, herbs, or cheeses to suit your taste preferences. An egg white omelette is a versatile and nutritious breakfast option that can be tailored to your liking. Enjoy!

Sweet Potato and Black Bean Chili

Ingredients:

- 1 tablespoon olive oil
- 1 large onion, diced
- 3 cloves garlic, minced
- 1 large sweet potato, peeled and diced
- 1 bell pepper, diced (any color)
- 1 can (15 oz) black beans, drained and rinsed
- 1 can (15 oz) diced tomatoes
- 1 can (15 oz) tomato sauce
- 1 cup vegetable broth
- 1 tablespoon chili powder
- 1 teaspoon ground cumin
- 1 teaspoon smoked paprika
- 1/2 teaspoon cinnamon
- Salt and pepper to taste
- Optional toppings: chopped green onions, cilantro, shredded cheese, sour cream

Instructions:

Sauté Vegetables: In a large pot, heat the olive oil over medium heat. Add the diced onion and cook until softened, about 3-4 minutes. Add the minced garlic and cook for an additional 1 minute.

Add Sweet Potato and Bell Pepper: Add the diced sweet potato and bell pepper to the pot. Cook for 5-7 minutes, stirring occasionally, until the vegetables start to soften.

Add Beans and Tomatoes: Stir in the black beans, diced tomatoes, tomato sauce, and vegetable broth.

Season: Add chili powder, ground cumin, smoked paprika, cinnamon, salt, and pepper. Stir well to combine.

Simmer: Bring the chili to a simmer, then reduce the heat to low, cover, and let it simmer for about 20-25 minutes or until the sweet potatoes are tender.

Adjust Seasoning: Taste and adjust the seasoning if needed.

Serve: Ladle the chili into bowls and garnish with chopped green onions, cilantro, shredded cheese, or sour cream if desired.

This Sweet Potato and Black Bean Chili is not only delicious but also packed with nutrients. It's a great option for a satisfying and healthy meal. Enjoy!

Shrimp and Avocado Salad

Ingredients:

For the Salad:

- 1 pound large shrimp, peeled and deveined
- 2 tablespoons olive oil
- Salt and pepper to taste
- 1 teaspoon smoked paprika
- 1 teaspoon garlic powder
- 8 cups mixed salad greens (e.g., spinach, arugula, romaine)
- 2 avocados, diced
- 1 cup cherry tomatoes, halved
- 1/2 red onion, thinly sliced

For the Dressing:

- 3 tablespoons extra-virgin olive oil
- 2 tablespoons lime juice
- 1 tablespoon honey
- 1 teaspoon Dijon mustard
- Salt and pepper to taste

Instructions:

Prepare Shrimp: In a bowl, toss the shrimp with olive oil, salt, pepper, smoked paprika, and garlic powder.

Cook Shrimp: Heat a skillet over medium-high heat. Add the shrimp and cook for 2-3 minutes per side or until they are pink and opaque. Remove from heat and set aside.

Make Dressing: In a small bowl, whisk together the extra-virgin olive oil, lime juice, honey, Dijon mustard, salt, and pepper. Set aside.

Assemble Salad: In a large salad bowl, combine the mixed greens, diced avocados, cherry tomatoes, and thinly sliced red onion.

Add Shrimp: Arrange the cooked shrimp on top of the salad.

Drizzle Dressing: Drizzle the dressing over the salad and toss gently to coat everything evenly.

Serve: Divide the salad onto plates and serve immediately.

This Shrimp and Avocado Salad is not only vibrant but also full of contrasting textures and flavors. It makes for a perfect light lunch or dinner option, especially during warmer seasons. Feel free to customize the salad with additional ingredients like cucumbers, feta cheese, or fresh herbs. Enjoy!

Roasted Brussels Sprouts

Ingredients:

- 1 pound Brussels sprouts, trimmed and halved
- 2 tablespoons olive oil
- Salt and pepper to taste
- Optional additions: minced garlic, grated Parmesan cheese, balsamic glaze, or chopped bacon

Instructions:

Preheat the Oven: Preheat your oven to 400°F (200°C).

Prepare Brussels Sprouts: Trim the ends of the Brussels sprouts and cut them in half. Remove any loose or damaged outer leaves.

Toss with Olive Oil: In a large bowl, toss the halved Brussels sprouts with olive oil until they are evenly coated.

Season: Sprinkle salt and pepper over the Brussels sprouts, adjusting to taste. If you like, you can add minced garlic or any other seasonings of your choice.

Spread on Baking Sheet: Arrange the Brussels sprouts in a single layer on a baking sheet. Make sure they are not too crowded to allow even roasting.

Roast in the Oven: Place the baking sheet in the preheated oven and roast for 20-25 minutes, or until the Brussels sprouts are golden brown and crispy on the edges. Shake the pan or toss the Brussels sprouts halfway through the cooking time for even roasting.

Optional Additions: If desired, sprinkle grated Parmesan cheese over the Brussels sprouts during the last 5 minutes of roasting. You can also drizzle balsamic glaze or add chopped cooked bacon for extra flavor.

Serve: Remove the roasted Brussels sprouts from the oven and transfer them to a serving dish. Serve hot.

Roasted Brussels sprouts are a versatile side dish that pairs well with various main courses. They are not only delicious but also a great source of vitamins and fiber. Enjoy your crispy and flavorful Brussels sprouts!

Lentil Soup

Ingredients:

- 1 cup dried lentils (green or brown), rinsed and drained
- 1 onion, finely chopped
- 2 carrots, diced
- 2 celery stalks, diced
- 3 cloves garlic, minced
- 1 can (14 oz) diced tomatoes (with juices)
- 6 cups vegetable or chicken broth
- 1 teaspoon ground cumin
- 1 teaspoon ground coriander
- 1 teaspoon smoked paprika
- 1 bay leaf
- Salt and pepper to taste
- 2 tablespoons olive oil
- Fresh lemon juice (optional, for serving)
- Fresh parsley or cilantro, chopped (for garnish)

Instructions:

Sauté Vegetables: In a large soup pot, heat olive oil over medium heat. Add chopped onion, carrots, and celery. Cook for about 5 minutes until the vegetables are softened.
Add Garlic and Spices: Add minced garlic, ground cumin, ground coriander, and smoked paprika. Sauté for an additional 1-2 minutes until fragrant.
Add Lentils and Tomatoes: Stir in the rinsed lentils, diced tomatoes (with juices), and bay leaf.
Pour in Broth: Pour in the vegetable or chicken broth. Bring the soup to a boil, then reduce the heat to low, cover, and let it simmer for about 25-30 minutes or until the lentils are tender.
Season: Season the soup with salt and pepper to taste. Adjust the seasoning if needed.
Serve: Remove the bay leaf and discard it. Ladle the lentil soup into bowls. Squeeze fresh lemon juice over each serving if desired.
Garnish: Garnish the soup with chopped fresh parsley or cilantro.

This lentil soup is not only delicious but also a great source of protein and fiber. Feel free to customize it by adding additional vegetables, spices, or even a splash of vinegar for extra acidity. Enjoy your warm and comforting bowl of lentil soup!

Cauliflower Rice Stir-Fry

Ingredients:

For Cauliflower Rice:

- 1 medium-sized cauliflower, washed and dried
- 1 tablespoon olive oil
- Salt and pepper to taste

For Stir-Fry:

- 2 tablespoons sesame oil
- 2 cloves garlic, minced
- 1 tablespoon ginger, grated
- 1 cup broccoli florets
- 1 carrot, julienned
- 1 bell pepper, thinly sliced (any color)
- 1 cup snap peas, ends trimmed
- 1 cup sliced mushrooms
- 1 cup cooked protein of your choice (tofu, chicken, shrimp, etc.)
- 3 tablespoons soy sauce
- 1 tablespoon rice vinegar
- 1 teaspoon honey or maple syrup (optional, for sweetness)
- Green onions, chopped, for garnish
- Sesame seeds, for garnish

Instructions:

Cauliflower Rice:

Prepare Cauliflower: Cut the cauliflower into florets, discarding the stems. Place the florets in a food processor and pulse until it resembles rice-sized granules. Cook Cauliflower Rice: Heat olive oil in a large skillet over medium heat. Add the cauliflower rice and sauté for 5-7 minutes, stirring occasionally, until it's tender but not mushy. Season with salt and pepper to taste. Set aside.

Stir-Fry:

Sauté Aromatics: In the same skillet, heat sesame oil over medium-high heat. Add minced garlic and grated ginger, sautéing for about 30 seconds until fragrant.

Add Vegetables: Add broccoli, julienned carrot, sliced bell pepper, snap peas, and sliced mushrooms. Stir-fry for 5-7 minutes until the vegetables are tender-crisp.

Add Protein: If using cooked protein (tofu, chicken, shrimp, etc.), add it to the skillet and toss until heated through.

Sauce: In a small bowl, mix soy sauce, rice vinegar, and honey or maple syrup if using. Pour the sauce over the stir-fry and toss to coat.

Combine with Cauliflower Rice: Add the cooked cauliflower rice to the skillet and toss until well combined and heated through.

Garnish and Serve: Garnish the cauliflower rice stir-fry with chopped green onions and sesame seeds. Serve hot.

This cauliflower rice stir-fry is a flavorful and nutritious option that can be customized with your favorite vegetables and protein. Enjoy your delicious and low-carb stir-fry!

Greek Salad

Ingredients:

- 4 cups cherry tomatoes, halved
- 1 cucumber, diced
- 1 red bell pepper, diced
- 1 red onion, thinly sliced
- 1 cup Kalamata olives, pitted
- 1 cup feta cheese, crumbled
- 1/2 cup fresh parsley, chopped
- 1/4 cup extra-virgin olive oil
- 2 tablespoons red wine vinegar
- 1 teaspoon dried oregano
- Salt and pepper to taste

Instructions:

Prepare Vegetables: In a large salad bowl, combine the cherry tomatoes, diced cucumber, diced red bell pepper, thinly sliced red onion, Kalamata olives, and crumbled feta cheese.
Make Dressing: In a small bowl, whisk together the extra-virgin olive oil, red wine vinegar, dried oregano, salt, and pepper. Adjust the seasoning to taste.
Toss Salad: Drizzle the dressing over the salad and toss gently to coat the vegetables and feta evenly.
Garnish: Sprinkle chopped fresh parsley over the salad as a garnish.
Serve: Serve immediately, or refrigerate for a short time before serving to let the flavors meld.

Optional Additions:

- Add diced or sliced cucumbers for extra crunch.
- Include green bell peppers or cherry tomatoes of different colors for a more colorful presentation.
- Top with grilled chicken, shrimp, or gyro slices for a protein boost.

This Greek salad is not only delicious but also a healthy option rich in vitamins, minerals, and antioxidants. Enjoy it as a refreshing side dish or add your favorite protein to make it a complete meal.

Turkey and Veggie Skewers

Ingredients:

- 1 pound turkey breast, cut into bite-sized cubes
- 1 zucchini, sliced
- 1 bell pepper (any color), cut into chunks
- 1 red onion, cut into chunks
- Cherry tomatoes
- 1/4 cup olive oil
- 2 tablespoons soy sauce
- 2 tablespoons Dijon mustard
- 2 cloves garlic, minced
- 1 teaspoon dried oregano
- 1 teaspoon paprika
- Salt and pepper to taste
- Wooden skewers, soaked in water for 30 minutes (if grilling)

Instructions:

Marinate Turkey: In a bowl, whisk together olive oil, soy sauce, Dijon mustard, minced garlic, dried oregano, paprika, salt, and pepper to create the marinade.
Thread Skewers: Place the turkey cubes and prepared vegetables in a large bowl. Pour the marinade over the turkey and vegetables, making sure everything is well-coated. Marinate for at least 30 minutes, or refrigerate for a few hours for better flavor.
Preheat Grill or Oven: If grilling, preheat your grill to medium-high heat. If baking, preheat your oven to 400°F (200°C).
Skewer Ingredients: Thread the marinated turkey and vegetables onto the skewers, alternating between turkey and veggies.
Grill or Bake: If grilling, place the skewers on the preheated grill and cook for about 10-15 minutes, turning occasionally, until the turkey is cooked through and the vegetables are tender. If baking, place the skewers on a baking sheet and bake in the preheated oven for 20-25 minutes or until done.
Serve: Remove the skewers from the grill or oven. Serve hot with your favorite side dishes.

These turkey and veggie skewers are not only flavorful but also a great way to incorporate lean protein and a variety of vegetables into your meal. Enjoy this dish as a healthy and satisfying option for lunch or dinner!

Baked Cod with Herbs

Ingredients:

- 4 cod fillets (about 6 ounces each)
- 2 tablespoons olive oil
- 2 tablespoons fresh lemon juice
- 2 cloves garlic, minced
- 1 teaspoon dried oregano
- 1 teaspoon dried thyme
- 1 teaspoon dried rosemary
- Salt and pepper to taste
- Lemon wedges for serving
- Fresh parsley, chopped, for garnish

Instructions:

Preheat Oven: Preheat your oven to 400°F (200°C).
Prepare Cod Fillets: Pat the cod fillets dry with paper towels and place them in a baking dish.
Make Herb Marinade: In a small bowl, whisk together olive oil, fresh lemon juice, minced garlic, dried oregano, dried thyme, dried rosemary, salt, and pepper.
Coat Cod with Marinade: Pour the herb marinade over the cod fillets, making sure they are evenly coated. You can use a brush or your hands to ensure the fillets are covered with the mixture.
Bake Cod: Bake in the preheated oven for 12-15 minutes or until the cod is opaque and flakes easily with a fork.
Broil for Crispiness (Optional): If you want a golden and slightly crispy top, you can turn on the broiler for the last 1-2 minutes of baking.
Garnish and Serve: Remove the cod from the oven, garnish with fresh chopped parsley, and serve hot. Optionally, serve with lemon wedges on the side for extra flavor.

This baked cod with herbs is not only delicious but also a healthy option. You can pair it with steamed vegetables, quinoa, or a side salad for a well-balanced meal. Enjoy your flavorful and nutritious dish!

Spinach and Feta Stuffed Chicken Breast

Ingredients:

- 4 boneless, skinless chicken breasts
- 2 cups fresh spinach, chopped
- 1/2 cup feta cheese, crumbled
- 2 tablespoons olive oil
- 2 cloves garlic, minced
- 1 teaspoon dried oregano
- Salt and pepper to taste
- Toothpicks or kitchen twine
- Lemon wedges for serving (optional)

Instructions:

Preheat Oven: Preheat your oven to 375°F (190°C).
Prepare Chicken Breasts: Lay the chicken breasts flat on a cutting board. Using a sharp knife, make a horizontal cut along the thicker side of each chicken breast to create a pocket without cutting through the other side.
Make Filling: In a skillet, heat olive oil over medium heat. Add minced garlic and sauté until fragrant. Add chopped spinach and cook until wilted. Remove from heat and let it cool slightly. Stir in crumbled feta, dried oregano, salt, and pepper.
Stuff Chicken: Stuff each chicken breast pocket with the spinach and feta mixture. Use toothpicks or kitchen twine to secure the openings and keep the filling in place.
Season and Sear: Season the outside of the chicken breasts with salt and pepper. In an oven-safe skillet, heat a bit of olive oil over medium-high heat. Sear the stuffed chicken breasts for 2-3 minutes per side, or until golden brown.
Finish in the Oven: Transfer the skillet to the preheated oven and bake for 20-25 minutes or until the chicken is cooked through and reaches an internal temperature of 165°F (74°C).
Serve: Remove toothpicks or twine before serving. Optionally, squeeze fresh lemon juice over the stuffed chicken breasts before serving.
Garnish and Enjoy: Garnish with additional fresh herbs if desired. Serve hot and enjoy your Spinach and Feta Stuffed Chicken Breast!

This dish pairs well with a side of roasted vegetables, quinoa, or a light salad. It's a perfect choice for a special dinner or when you want to impress with a delicious and visually appealing meal.

Mushroom and Spinach Quiche (with Egg Whites)

Ingredients:

For the Crust:

- 1 pre-made or homemade pie crust (9 inches)

For the Filling:

- 2 cups fresh spinach, chopped
- 1 cup mushrooms, sliced
- 1 small onion, finely chopped
- 1 clove garlic, minced
- 1 tablespoon olive oil
- 1 cup shredded Swiss or Gruyere cheese
- 6 large egg whites
- 1 cup low-fat milk or almond milk
- Salt and pepper to taste
- 1/4 teaspoon nutmeg (optional)

Instructions:

Preheat Oven: Preheat your oven to 375°F (190°C).
Prepare Crust: If using a pre-made pie crust, place it in a 9-inch pie dish according to package instructions. If making a homemade crust, prepare and blind-bake it for 8-10 minutes until lightly golden.
Sauté Vegetables: In a skillet, heat olive oil over medium heat. Add chopped onions and cook until softened. Add minced garlic, sliced mushrooms, and chopped spinach. Cook until the mushrooms release their moisture and the spinach is wilted. Remove from heat and let it cool slightly.
Prepare Filling: In a bowl, whisk together the egg whites, milk, shredded cheese, salt, pepper, and nutmeg (if using). Add the sautéed vegetable mixture to the bowl and mix well.
Assemble Quiche: Pour the filling into the prepared pie crust.
Bake: Place the quiche in the preheated oven and bake for 35-40 minutes or until the center is set and the top is golden brown.
Cool and Serve: Allow the quiche to cool for a few minutes before slicing. Serve warm.

Optional Garnish: Garnish with additional fresh herbs or a sprinkle of cheese if desired.

This Mushroom and Spinach Quiche with egg whites is a delicious and nutritious option for brunch or a light dinner. Feel free to customize the filling by adding other vegetables or herbs according to your taste. Enjoy your flavorful and healthier quiche!

Cucumber and Tomato Salad

Ingredients:

- 2 cucumbers, thinly sliced
- 4 medium-sized tomatoes, diced
- 1/2 red onion, thinly sliced
- 1/4 cup fresh parsley, chopped
- 2 tablespoons fresh mint, chopped (optional)
- 1/4 cup extra-virgin olive oil
- 2 tablespoons red wine vinegar
- Salt and pepper to taste
- Feta cheese, crumbled (optional)

Instructions:

Prepare Vegetables: In a large bowl, combine the thinly sliced cucumbers, diced tomatoes, thinly sliced red onion, chopped parsley, and mint.
Make Dressing: In a small bowl, whisk together the extra-virgin olive oil and red wine vinegar. Season with salt and pepper to taste.
Combine: Pour the dressing over the cucumber and tomato mixture. Toss everything gently to coat the vegetables evenly.
Refrigerate: Cover the bowl and refrigerate for at least 30 minutes to allow the flavors to meld.
Optional Garnish: Before serving, you can sprinkle crumbled feta cheese over the top for an extra burst of flavor.
Serve: Serve the cucumber and tomato salad chilled as a refreshing side dish.

This salad is not only easy to make but also a great way to enjoy the flavors of fresh, seasonal vegetables. It complements grilled meats, fish, or can be enjoyed on its own. Customize it with your favorite herbs or add olives for additional flavor. Enjoy your crisp and vibrant cucumber and tomato salad!

Oven-Baked Turkey Meatballs

Ingredients:

For the Meatballs:

- 1 pound ground turkey
- 1/2 cup breadcrumbs (whole wheat or panko)
- 1/4 cup grated Parmesan cheese
- 1/4 cup fresh parsley, chopped
- 1/4 cup onion, finely minced
- 2 cloves garlic, minced
- 1 large egg
- 1 teaspoon dried oregano
- 1 teaspoon dried basil
- 1/2 teaspoon salt
- 1/4 teaspoon black pepper

For the Sauce:

- 2 cups marinara sauce (store-bought or homemade)

Instructions:

Preheat Oven: Preheat your oven to 400°F (200°C). Line a baking sheet with parchment paper.
Prepare Meatball Mixture: In a large bowl, combine ground turkey, breadcrumbs, grated Parmesan cheese, chopped parsley, minced onion, minced garlic, egg, dried oregano, dried basil, salt, and black pepper. Mix until well combined.
Form Meatballs: Using your hands, shape the mixture into meatballs, about 1 to 1.5 inches in diameter. Place the meatballs on the prepared baking sheet.
Bake Meatballs: Bake in the preheated oven for 20-25 minutes or until the meatballs are cooked through and browned on the outside. You can turn them halfway through the cooking time for even browning.
Warm Sauce: While the meatballs are baking, warm the marinara sauce in a saucepan over medium heat.

Combine and Serve: Once the meatballs are done, transfer them to the saucepan with the warmed marinara sauce. Gently coat the meatballs with the sauce.
Serve: Serve the turkey meatballs with sauce over pasta, rice, or on a sub roll for a meatball sandwich.

Feel free to garnish with additional grated Parmesan cheese and chopped parsley before serving. These oven-baked turkey meatballs are a healthier option and can be enjoyed in various ways. They also freeze well, making them a convenient option for future meals. Enjoy your tasty and lean turkey meatballs!

Broccoli and Cheddar Stuffed Potatoes

Ingredients:

- 4 large baking potatoes
- 2 cups broccoli florets, steamed or blanched
- 1 cup sharp cheddar cheese, shredded
- 1/2 cup sour cream
- 2 tablespoons butter
- 2 green onions, thinly sliced
- Salt and pepper to taste
- Optional toppings: additional shredded cheese, chopped bacon, chopped chives

Instructions:

Preheat Oven: Preheat your oven to 400°F (200°C).
Bake Potatoes: Scrub the potatoes clean and pierce each one several times with a fork. Place them directly on the oven rack and bake for about 45-60 minutes or until they are tender when pierced with a fork.
Prepare Broccoli: While the potatoes are baking, steam or blanch the broccoli until it is just tender. Chop the broccoli into small florets.
Cut and Scoop Potatoes: Once the potatoes are done, remove them from the oven and let them cool slightly. Cut each potato in half lengthwise. Carefully scoop out most of the potato flesh, leaving a thin shell.
Mash Potato Flesh: In a bowl, mash the scooped-out potato flesh with butter, sour cream, salt, and pepper. Mix until smooth.
Combine with Broccoli and Cheese: Add the steamed broccoli, shredded cheddar cheese, and sliced green onions to the mashed potatoes. Mix until well combined.
Refill Potato Shells: Spoon the broccoli and cheese mixture back into the potato shells.
Bake Again: Place the stuffed potatoes back in the oven and bake for an additional 10-15 minutes, or until the cheese is melted and bubbly.
Serve: Remove from the oven and let them cool for a few minutes. Optionally, top with additional shredded cheese, chopped bacon, and chopped chives before serving.

These Broccoli and Cheddar Stuffed Potatoes are a comforting and flavorful dish. They can be served as a side dish or as a main course with a side salad. Customize them with your favorite toppings and enjoy a satisfying meal!

Sesame Ginger Tofu Stir-Fry

Ingredients:

For the Tofu:

- 1 block extra-firm tofu, pressed and cubed
- 2 tablespoons soy sauce
- 1 tablespoon sesame oil
- 1 tablespoon cornstarch

For the Stir-Fry:

- 2 tablespoons vegetable oil
- 1 tablespoon fresh ginger, minced
- 2 cloves garlic, minced
- 1 bell pepper, thinly sliced
- 1 carrot, julienned
- 1 cup broccoli florets
- 1 cup snap peas, ends trimmed
- 2 tablespoons soy sauce
- 1 tablespoon hoisin sauce
- 1 tablespoon rice vinegar
- 1 tablespoon sesame oil
- 1 tablespoon maple syrup or honey
- 1 teaspoon cornstarch mixed with 2 teaspoons water (optional, for thickening)
- Sesame seeds for garnish (optional)
- Green onions, chopped, for garnish

Instructions:

Prepare Tofu:

> Preheat your oven to 400°F (200°C).
> In a bowl, mix together soy sauce, sesame oil, and cornstarch.
> Toss the cubed tofu in the soy sauce mixture until evenly coated.

Place the tofu on a baking sheet lined with parchment paper. Bake for 25-30 minutes or until the tofu is golden and crispy, flipping halfway through.

Prepare Stir-Fry:

In a large wok or skillet, heat vegetable oil over medium-high heat.
Add minced ginger and garlic, sauté for about 30 seconds until fragrant.
Add bell pepper, julienned carrot, broccoli florets, and snap peas. Stir-fry for 3-5 minutes or until the vegetables are crisp-tender.
In a small bowl, whisk together soy sauce, hoisin sauce, rice vinegar, sesame oil, and maple syrup (or honey).
Add the baked tofu to the stir-fry and pour the sauce over the tofu and vegetables. Toss everything to coat evenly.
If you prefer a thicker sauce, you can mix cornstarch with water to create a slurry and add it to the stir-fry. Cook for an additional minute until the sauce thickens.
Garnish with sesame seeds and chopped green onions.
Serve the Sesame Ginger Tofu Stir-Fry over rice or noodles.

Enjoy this flavorful and nutritious Sesame Ginger Tofu Stir-Fry! Adjust the sauce ingredients to your taste preferences, and feel free to add more vegetables or customize it with your favorite stir-fry ingredients.

Chickpea Salad

Ingredients:

- 2 cans (15 oz each) chickpeas, drained and rinsed
- 1 cucumber, diced
- 1 bell pepper (any color), diced
- 1 cup cherry tomatoes, halved
- 1/2 red onion, finely chopped
- 1/4 cup fresh parsley, chopped
- 1/4 cup feta cheese, crumbled (optional)
- 1/4 cup Kalamata olives, pitted and sliced (optional)

For the Dressing:

- 1/4 cup extra-virgin olive oil
- 2 tablespoons red wine vinegar
- 1 clove garlic, minced
- 1 teaspoon Dijon mustard
- 1 teaspoon honey or maple syrup
- Salt and pepper to taste

Instructions:

Prepare Chickpeas: In a large bowl, combine the drained and rinsed chickpeas.
Add Vegetables: Add diced cucumber, diced bell pepper, cherry tomatoes, finely chopped red onion, and chopped fresh parsley to the bowl.
Optional Additions: If desired, add crumbled feta cheese and sliced Kalamata olives for extra flavor.
Make Dressing: In a small bowl, whisk together extra-virgin olive oil, red wine vinegar, minced garlic, Dijon mustard, honey or maple syrup, salt, and pepper.
Toss Salad: Pour the dressing over the chickpea and vegetable mixture. Toss everything gently to coat evenly.
Chill and Marinate: Cover the bowl and refrigerate the chickpea salad for at least 30 minutes to allow the flavors to meld.
Serve: Before serving, give the salad a quick toss. Adjust the seasoning if needed.

This chickpea salad is not only delicious but also a great source of protein and fiber. Enjoy it as a light and refreshing meal on its own or as a side dish alongside grilled chicken or fish. Feel free to customize the salad with additional vegetables, herbs, or your favorite dressing.

Baked Chicken with Rosemary

Ingredients:

- 4 bone-in, skin-on chicken thighs
- 2 tablespoons olive oil
- 2 teaspoons fresh rosemary, chopped (or 1 teaspoon dried rosemary)
- 4 cloves garlic, minced
- 1 teaspoon lemon zest
- 1 tablespoon lemon juice
- Salt and pepper to taste
- 1 lemon, sliced (for garnish, optional)

Instructions:

Preheat Oven: Preheat your oven to 400°F (200°C).
Prepare Chicken: Pat the chicken thighs dry with paper towels. Season both sides with salt and pepper.
Make Rosemary Marinade: In a small bowl, mix together olive oil, chopped rosemary, minced garlic, lemon zest, and lemon juice.
Coat Chicken: Brush the chicken thighs with the rosemary marinade, making sure to coat them evenly.
Bake: Place the chicken thighs on a baking sheet lined with parchment paper or in a baking dish. If desired, place lemon slices under and around the chicken for added flavor. Bake in the preheated oven for 30-35 minutes or until the chicken reaches an internal temperature of 165°F (74°C) and the skin is crispy.
Broil (Optional): If you want the skin to be extra crispy, you can broil the chicken for an additional 2-3 minutes, keeping a close eye to prevent burning.
Rest and Serve: Let the chicken rest for a few minutes before serving to allow the juices to redistribute. Garnish with additional fresh rosemary and lemon slices if desired.
Serve: Serve the baked chicken with rosemary alongside your favorite side dishes.

This baked chicken with rosemary is a simple and elegant dish that's perfect for a weeknight dinner or a special occasion. The combination of rosemary and citrus adds a delightful and aromatic flavor to the chicken. Enjoy your delicious and herb-infused baked chicken!

Zucchini Noodles with Pesto

Ingredients:

For Zucchini Noodles:

- 4 medium-sized zucchini, spiralized or julienned
- Salt for sprinkling

For Pesto Sauce:

- 2 cups fresh basil leaves, packed
- 1/2 cup grated Parmesan cheese
- 1/2 cup pine nuts or walnuts
- 2 cloves garlic, peeled
- 1/2 cup extra-virgin olive oil
- Salt and pepper to taste
- Juice of half a lemon (optional)

Optional Toppings:

- Cherry tomatoes, halved
- Extra Parmesan cheese
- Fresh basil leaves

Instructions:

Prepare Zucchini Noodles:

Spiralize or julienne the zucchini into noodle-like shapes.
Sprinkle the zucchini noodles with salt and let them sit in a colander for about 15-20 minutes. This helps draw out excess moisture. Afterward, pat them dry with a paper towel.

Make Pesto Sauce:

In a food processor, combine basil leaves, grated Parmesan cheese, pine nuts or walnuts, and garlic cloves.

Pulse the ingredients until coarsely chopped.

With the food processor running, slowly drizzle in the olive oil until the pesto reaches your desired consistency. You may need to stop and scrape down the sides of the bowl.

Season the pesto with salt and pepper to taste. Add lemon juice if desired for a citrusy kick.

Assemble Zucchini Noodles with Pesto:

In a large bowl, toss the zucchini noodles with the prepared pesto until well coated.

Optional: Top with cherry tomatoes, extra Parmesan cheese, and fresh basil leaves.

Serve immediately and enjoy your zucchini noodles with pesto!

This dish is not only delicious but also a great way to incorporate more vegetables into your diet. It's a quick and flavorful option for a light lunch or dinner. Customize it by adding grilled chicken, shrimp, or any other protein of your choice if you'd like.

Salmon and Asparagus Foil Packets

Ingredients:

- 4 salmon fillets
- 1 bunch asparagus, tough ends trimmed
- 4 tablespoons olive oil
- 4 cloves garlic, minced
- 1 lemon, sliced
- 4 teaspoons Dijon mustard
- Salt and pepper to taste
- Fresh herbs (such as dill, parsley, or thyme) for garnish

Instructions:

Preheat Oven: Preheat your oven to 400°F (200°C).
Prepare Foil Packets: Cut four large pieces of aluminum foil. Place a salmon fillet in the center of each piece of foil.
Season Salmon: Season each salmon fillet with salt and pepper. Brush each fillet with 1 teaspoon of Dijon mustard.
Add Asparagus: Divide the asparagus evenly among the foil packets, arranging them next to the salmon.
Drizzle with Olive Oil: Drizzle each salmon fillet and asparagus with 1 tablespoon of olive oil. Sprinkle minced garlic over the top.
Add Lemon Slices: Place a couple of lemon slices on each salmon fillet.
Wrap and Seal: Fold the sides of the foil over the salmon and asparagus, sealing the edges tightly to create a packet.
Bake: Place the foil packets on a baking sheet and bake in the preheated oven for 15-20 minutes, or until the salmon is cooked through and flakes easily with a fork.
Garnish and Serve: Carefully open the foil packets, garnish with fresh herbs, and serve immediately.

This method of cooking keeps the salmon moist and allows the flavors to meld together. You can also customize the recipe by adding additional seasonings or vegetables of your choice. Enjoy your easy and flavorful salmon and asparagus foil packets!

Tomato Basil Soup

Ingredients:

- 2 tablespoons olive oil
- 1 onion, chopped
- 2 cloves garlic, minced
- 2 cans (28 oz each) whole peeled tomatoes
- 1 can (14 oz) crushed tomatoes
- 4 cups vegetable or chicken broth
- 1 teaspoon sugar (optional, to balance acidity)
- Salt and pepper to taste
- 1/2 cup fresh basil leaves, chopped
- 1/2 cup heavy cream or half-and-half (optional, for a creamier soup)
- Grated Parmesan cheese for garnish (optional)
- Croutons or bread for serving

Instructions:

Sauté Onion and Garlic:
- In a large pot, heat olive oil over medium heat. Add chopped onions and sauté until translucent. Add minced garlic and cook for an additional 1-2 minutes until fragrant.

Add Tomatoes:
- Pour in the whole peeled tomatoes and crushed tomatoes, breaking up the whole tomatoes with a spoon. Stir to combine.

Simmer:
- Add vegetable or chicken broth, sugar (if using), salt, and pepper. Bring the mixture to a simmer, then reduce the heat and let it simmer for about 20-25 minutes, allowing the flavors to meld.

Blend Soup:
- Use an immersion blender to blend the soup until smooth. Alternatively, transfer the soup in batches to a blender and blend until smooth. Be cautious as hot liquids can splatter.

Add Basil and Cream:
- Stir in the chopped basil and, if desired, add heavy cream or half-and-half for a creamier texture. Simmer for an additional 5-10 minutes.

Adjust Seasoning:

- Taste the soup and adjust the seasoning as needed. Add more salt, pepper, or sugar to achieve the desired balance.

Serve:
- Ladle the soup into bowls. Garnish with grated Parmesan cheese, additional fresh basil, and serve with croutons or a slice of bread.

Enjoy your homemade tomato basil soup! This classic recipe is perfect for a cozy meal, and you can easily customize it to suit your taste preferences.

Asian-Inspired Cabbage Rolls

Ingredients:

For the Cabbage Rolls:

- 1 large head of cabbage
- 1 pound ground pork or chicken
- 1 cup cooked rice (white or brown)
- 1 cup shiitake mushrooms, finely chopped
- 1/2 cup water chestnuts, finely chopped
- 1/4 cup green onions, finely chopped
- 2 cloves garlic, minced
- 1 tablespoon fresh ginger, grated
- 2 tablespoons soy sauce
- 1 tablespoon oyster sauce
- 1 teaspoon sesame oil
- Salt and pepper to taste

For the Sauce:

- 1/2 cup soy sauce
- 2 tablespoons hoisin sauce
- 1 tablespoon rice vinegar
- 1 tablespoon brown sugar
- 1 teaspoon sesame oil
- 1 teaspoon cornstarch (optional, for thickening)

Instructions:

Prepare the Cabbage:

　Boil Cabbage Leaves:
  - Bring a large pot of water to a boil. Carefully remove the core from the cabbage head and place it in the boiling water. As the leaves loosen, carefully peel them off. Cook for about 2-3 minutes or until softened. Drain and set aside.

Make the Filling:

- Cook Ground Meat:
  - In a large skillet, cook the ground pork or chicken over medium heat until browned. Drain excess fat if necessary.
- Add Vegetables and Flavorings:
  - Add shiitake mushrooms, water chestnuts, green onions, minced garlic, grated ginger, soy sauce, oyster sauce, sesame oil, salt, and pepper to the skillet. Cook for an additional 3-4 minutes until the vegetables are tender.
- Combine with Rice:
  - Stir in the cooked rice and mix until well combined. Remove from heat.

Assemble and Cook:

- Fill Cabbage Leaves:
  - Place a spoonful of the filling in the center of each cabbage leaf. Fold the sides over the filling and roll up tightly.
- Place in Baking Dish:
  - Arrange the cabbage rolls in a baking dish, seam side down.

Prepare the Sauce:

- Mix Sauce Ingredients:
  - In a bowl, whisk together soy sauce, hoisin sauce, rice vinegar, brown sugar, and sesame oil. If you prefer a thicker sauce, you can add cornstarch dissolved in a little water.
- Pour Sauce Over Cabbage Rolls:
  - Pour the sauce over the cabbage rolls, ensuring they are well-coated.
- Bake:
  - Bake in a preheated oven at 350°F (175°C) for 25-30 minutes or until the cabbage rolls are heated through.
- Serve:
  - Serve the Asian-inspired cabbage rolls hot, garnished with additional chopped green onions or sesame seeds if desired.

These Asian-inspired cabbage rolls are a delicious and flavorful alternative to the traditional version. Enjoy the fusion of ingredients and the unique taste of these rolls!

Mango Avocado Quinoa Bowl

Ingredients:

For the Quinoa:

- 1 cup quinoa, rinsed
- 2 cups water or vegetable broth
- 1/4 teaspoon salt

For the Bowl:

- 1 ripe mango, peeled, pitted, and diced
- 1 ripe avocado, peeled, pitted, and sliced
- 1 cup cherry tomatoes, halved
- 1/4 cup red onion, finely chopped
- 1/4 cup fresh cilantro, chopped
- 1/4 cup feta cheese, crumbled (optional)

For the Dressing:

- 3 tablespoons extra-virgin olive oil
- 2 tablespoons lime juice
- 1 teaspoon honey or maple syrup
- Salt and pepper to taste

Instructions:

Prepare Quinoa:

Rinse Quinoa:
- Rinse quinoa under cold water.

Cook Quinoa:
- In a saucepan, combine quinoa, water or vegetable broth, and salt. Bring to a boil, then reduce the heat to low, cover, and simmer for 15-20 minutes, or until the quinoa is cooked and water is absorbed. Fluff with a fork and let it cool.

Assemble the Bowl:

Combine Ingredients:
- In a large bowl, combine the cooked quinoa, diced mango, sliced avocado, cherry tomatoes, chopped red onion, fresh cilantro, and crumbled feta cheese.

Prepare the Dressing:

Whisk Dressing:
- In a small bowl, whisk together extra-virgin olive oil, lime juice, honey or maple syrup, salt, and pepper.

Pour Dressing:
- Pour the dressing over the quinoa mixture and toss everything gently to coat.

Adjust Seasoning:
- Taste and adjust the seasoning as needed. Add more salt, pepper, or lime juice if desired.

Serve:

Divide into Bowls:
- Divide the Mango Avocado Quinoa mixture into serving bowls.

Garnish:
- Optionally, garnish with additional cilantro and feta cheese.

Enjoy:
- Serve the Mango Avocado Quinoa Bowl immediately and enjoy this fresh and flavorful dish!

This quinoa bowl is not only delicious but also packed with nutrients. It's a versatile recipe, and you can customize it by adding other ingredients like grilled chicken, shrimp, or your favorite vegetables. Enjoy the vibrant and wholesome flavors of this Mango Avocado Quinoa Bowl!

Herb-Roasted Vegetables

Ingredients:

- 4 cups mixed vegetables, such as carrots, potatoes, bell peppers, zucchini, and cherry tomatoes, cut into bite-sized pieces
- 3 tablespoons olive oil
- 2 cloves garlic, minced
- 1 teaspoon dried thyme
- 1 teaspoon dried rosemary
- 1 teaspoon dried oregano
- Salt and pepper to taste
- Fresh herbs for garnish, such as parsley or thyme (optional)

Instructions:

Preheat Oven:
- Preheat your oven to 425°F (220°C).

Prepare Vegetables:
- In a large bowl, toss the mixed vegetables with olive oil, minced garlic, dried thyme, dried rosemary, dried oregano, salt, and pepper. Make sure the vegetables are well coated.

Spread on Baking Sheet:
- Spread the seasoned vegetables in a single layer on a baking sheet. You can line the sheet with parchment paper for easy cleanup.

Roast:
- Roast in the preheated oven for 25-30 minutes or until the vegetables are tender and golden brown. Stir the vegetables halfway through the roasting time for even cooking.

Garnish and Serve:
- Once the vegetables are done, remove them from the oven and garnish with fresh herbs if desired.

Adjust Seasoning:
- Taste the roasted vegetables and adjust the seasoning if needed. Add more salt or pepper according to your preference.

Serve:
- Serve the herb-roasted vegetables as a side dish with your favorite main course.

This herb-roasted vegetable dish is not only delicious but also versatile. You can customize the herb blend based on your preferences. Additionally, you can experiment with different vegetables to suit your taste. Enjoy these flavorful and nutritious roasted vegetables with your meals!

Stuffed Bell Peppers with Turkey and Brown Rice

Ingredients:

- 4 large bell peppers, any color
- 1 pound ground turkey
- 1 cup cooked brown rice
- 1 cup black beans, drained and rinsed
- 1 cup corn kernels (fresh, frozen, or canned)
- 1 cup diced tomatoes
- 1/2 cup onion, finely chopped
- 2 cloves garlic, minced
- 1 teaspoon ground cumin
- 1 teaspoon chili powder
- 1/2 teaspoon paprika
- Salt and pepper to taste
- 1 cup shredded cheddar or Mexican blend cheese
- Fresh cilantro or green onions for garnish (optional)

Instructions:

Preheat Oven:
- Preheat your oven to 375°F (190°C).

Prepare Bell Peppers:
- Cut the tops off the bell peppers and remove the seeds and membranes. If needed, trim the bottoms of the peppers to help them stand upright in the baking dish.

Parboil Bell Peppers:
- Bring a large pot of water to boil. Submerge the bell peppers in the boiling water for about 3-4 minutes to soften slightly. Drain and set aside.

Cook Turkey and Vegetables:
- In a large skillet, cook the ground turkey over medium heat until browned. Add chopped onion and minced garlic and cook until the onion is softened.

Add Seasonings and Vegetables:
- Stir in ground cumin, chili powder, paprika, salt, and pepper. Add diced tomatoes, black beans, corn, and cooked brown rice. Mix well and cook for an additional 5 minutes until the mixture is heated through.

Fill Bell Peppers:

- Spoon the turkey and vegetable mixture into the parboiled bell peppers, pressing down gently to pack the filling.

Top with Cheese:

- Sprinkle shredded cheese on top of each stuffed pepper.

Bake:

- Place the stuffed peppers in a baking dish. Bake in the preheated oven for 25-30 minutes or until the peppers are tender and the cheese is melted and bubbly.

Garnish and Serve:

- Remove from the oven and let them cool slightly. Garnish with fresh cilantro or green onions if desired. Serve the stuffed bell peppers warm.

These stuffed bell peppers are not only delicious but also a great way to incorporate a variety of vegetables into your meal. Feel free to customize the filling with your favorite ingredients and spices. Enjoy your wholesome and flavorful turkey and brown rice stuffed bell peppers!

Garlic and Lemon Shrimp Skewers

Ingredients:

- 1 pound large shrimp, peeled and deveined
- 3 cloves garlic, minced
- Zest of 1 lemon
- Juice of 1 lemon
- 3 tablespoons olive oil
- 1 teaspoon dried oregano
- 1 teaspoon paprika
- Salt and pepper to taste
- Wooden or metal skewers
- Lemon wedges for serving

Instructions:

Prepare Shrimp:
- If using wooden skewers, soak them in water for about 30 minutes to prevent burning during grilling.

Marinate Shrimp:
- In a bowl, combine minced garlic, lemon zest, lemon juice, olive oil, dried oregano, paprika, salt, and pepper. Mix well to create the marinade.

Marinate Shrimp:
- Add the peeled and deveined shrimp to the marinade, making sure they are well coated. Allow the shrimp to marinate for at least 15-20 minutes, or you can refrigerate for up to 1 hour for more flavor.

Skewer Shrimp:
- Preheat your grill or grill pan to medium-high heat. Thread the marinated shrimp onto the skewers, ensuring they are evenly distributed.

Grill Shrimp:
- Grill the shrimp skewers for 2-3 minutes per side or until the shrimp are opaque and cooked through. Be careful not to overcook as shrimp can become rubbery.

Serve:
- Remove the shrimp skewers from the grill and serve immediately with lemon wedges on the side.

These garlic and lemon shrimp skewers are perfect as an appetizer or main dish. You can serve them over a bed of rice, quinoa, or a fresh salad. Customize the marinade with your favorite herbs and spices for additional flavor. Enjoy the bright and zesty taste of these grilled shrimp skewers!

Pesto Zoodles with Cherry Tomatoes

Ingredients:

- 4 medium-sized zucchini, spiralized
- 1 cup cherry tomatoes, halved
- 1/2 cup fresh basil leaves
- 1/3 cup pine nuts
- 1/3 cup grated Parmesan cheese
- 2 cloves garlic
- 1/2 cup extra-virgin olive oil
- Salt and pepper to taste
- Optional: Red pepper flakes for a hint of heat
- Optional: Additional grated Parmesan for serving

Instructions:

Prepare Zoodles:
- Use a spiralizer to turn the zucchini into noodles (zoodles). If you don't have a spiralizer, you can use a vegetable peeler to create thin strips.

Make Pesto:
- In a food processor, combine fresh basil, pine nuts, grated Parmesan, and garlic. Pulse until the ingredients are finely chopped.

Add Olive Oil:
- With the food processor running, slowly drizzle in the olive oil until the pesto reaches your desired consistency. Add salt and pepper to taste. If you like a bit of heat, you can add red pepper flakes.

Toss Zoodles:
- In a large pan, heat a small amount of olive oil over medium heat. Add the zoodles and cook for 2-3 minutes, just until they are heated through but still slightly firm.

Combine with Pesto:
- Add the cherry tomatoes to the pan and toss with the zoodles. Pour the pesto over the zoodles and cherry tomatoes, stirring until everything is well coated and heated through.

Serve:
- Remove from heat and serve the pesto zoodles with cherry tomatoes immediately. Optionally, garnish with additional grated Parmesan.

This Pesto Zoodles with Cherry Tomatoes recipe is not only delicious but also a low-carb and gluten-free alternative to traditional pasta. It's a quick and easy way to enjoy a light and flavorful dish. Feel free to customize the recipe with your favorite herbs or additional vegetables. Enjoy your healthy and tasty pesto zoodles!

Cauliflower and Broccoli Soup

Ingredients:

- 1 medium head of cauliflower, chopped into florets
- 2 cups broccoli florets
- 1 onion, chopped
- 2 cloves garlic, minced
- 4 cups vegetable or chicken broth
- 1 cup milk (dairy or plant-based)
- 2 tablespoons butter or olive oil
- Salt and pepper to taste
- 1 teaspoon dried thyme
- 1/2 teaspoon nutmeg (optional, for added flavor)
- 1/4 cup heavy cream (optional, for extra creaminess)
- Grated cheddar cheese for garnish (optional)
- Fresh parsley for garnish (optional)

Instructions:

Sauté Vegetables:
- In a large pot, heat butter or olive oil over medium heat. Add chopped onion and minced garlic. Sauté until the onion is translucent.

Add Cauliflower and Broccoli:
- Add cauliflower and broccoli florets to the pot. Cook for 5-7 minutes, stirring occasionally.

Pour in Broth:
- Pour in the vegetable or chicken broth. Bring the mixture to a boil, then reduce the heat to simmer. Cover the pot and let it simmer for about 15-20 minutes or until the vegetables are tender.

Blend Soup:
- Use an immersion blender to blend the soup until smooth. Alternatively, transfer the soup in batches to a blender and blend until smooth. Be cautious as hot liquids can splatter.

Add Milk and Seasonings:
- Stir in the milk, dried thyme, nutmeg (if using), salt, and pepper. Simmer for an additional 5-7 minutes.

Optional Creaminess:

- If you want an extra creamy texture, stir in the heavy cream.

Adjust Seasoning:
- Taste the soup and adjust the seasoning according to your preference.

Serve:
- Ladle the cauliflower and broccoli soup into bowls. Garnish with grated cheddar cheese and fresh parsley if desired.

This cauliflower and broccoli soup is not only delicious but also a great way to incorporate more vegetables into your diet. Enjoy it as a comforting and nutritious meal, especially during colder days!

Lemon Garlic Roasted Chicken

Ingredients:

- 1 whole chicken (about 3-4 pounds)
- 1 lemon, thinly sliced
- 6 cloves garlic, minced
- 2 tablespoons fresh rosemary, chopped
- 2 tablespoons fresh thyme, chopped
- 1/4 cup olive oil
- Salt and pepper to taste
- 1 cup chicken broth or white wine (optional)

Instructions:

Preheat Oven:
- Preheat your oven to 425°F (220°C).

Prepare Chicken:
- Pat the whole chicken dry with paper towels. Season the inside and outside of the chicken with salt and pepper.

Create Herb Mixture:
- In a small bowl, mix together minced garlic, chopped rosemary, chopped thyme, and olive oil to create a herb mixture.

Rub Chicken:
- Rub the herb mixture all over the chicken, ensuring it is evenly coated. Place a few lemon slices under the chicken skin for added flavor.

Stuff Chicken:
- Place some lemon slices inside the cavity of the chicken.

Tie Legs:
- If desired, tie the chicken legs together with kitchen twine for more even cooking.

Roast Chicken:
- Place the prepared chicken on a roasting rack in a roasting pan, breast side up. Roast in the preheated oven for about 1 hour or until the internal temperature reaches 165°F (74°C) and the skin is golden and crispy.

Baste (Optional):
- Optional: Baste the chicken with chicken broth or white wine every 20-30 minutes to keep it moist.

Rest and Serve:

- Remove the roasted chicken from the oven and let it rest for 10-15 minutes before carving. This allows the juices to redistribute.

Carve and Serve:
- Carve the chicken into serving pieces and serve with the roasted lemon slices.

This lemon garlic roasted chicken is a delicious and aromatic dish that's perfect for a family dinner or special occasion. The combination of lemon and garlic infuses the chicken with wonderful flavors. Enjoy your homemade roasted chicken!

Cucumber Roll-Ups with Hummus

Ingredients:

- 2 large cucumbers
- 1 cup hummus (store-bought or homemade)
- Cherry tomatoes, sliced (for garnish)
- Fresh parsley or dill, chopped (for garnish)

Instructions:

   Prepare Cucumbers:
   - Wash the cucumbers thoroughly. Using a vegetable peeler or a mandoline slicer, slice the cucumbers lengthwise into thin strips.

   Remove Excess Moisture:
   - Lay the cucumber strips on a paper towel to absorb excess moisture. This will help the hummus adhere better.

   Spread Hummus:
   - Spread a thin layer of hummus on each cucumber strip.

   Roll Up:
   - Starting from one end, roll up each cucumber strip with hummus into a tight spiral.

   Secure with Toothpick:
   - Secure the cucumber roll-up with a toothpick to hold it together.

   Garnish:
   - Garnish the cucumber roll-ups with sliced cherry tomatoes and chopped fresh parsley or dill.

   Chill (Optional):
   - For a cool and refreshing appetizer, you can chill the cucumber roll-ups in the refrigerator for 30 minutes before serving.

   Serve:
   - Arrange the cucumber roll-ups on a serving platter and serve as a light and healthy appetizer or snack.

These cucumber roll-ups with hummus are not only visually appealing but also a great gluten-free and low-carb alternative to traditional wraps. They're perfect for parties, picnics, or a quick and healthy snack. Feel free to customize the filling with additional veggies or herbs of your choice. Enjoy this light and flavorful treat!

Black Bean and Corn Salad

Ingredients:

- 2 cans (15 ounces each) black beans, drained and rinsed
- 2 cups frozen corn, thawed
- 1 red bell pepper, diced
- 1 orange or yellow bell pepper, diced
- 1 cup cherry tomatoes, halved
- 1/2 red onion, finely chopped
- 1/4 cup fresh cilantro, chopped
- 1 avocado, diced
- Juice of 2 limes
- 3 tablespoons extra-virgin olive oil
- 1 teaspoon ground cumin
- 1 teaspoon chili powder
- Salt and pepper to taste
- Optional: Jalapeño pepper, seeded and minced (for heat)

Instructions:

Prepare Vegetables:
- In a large bowl, combine black beans, thawed corn, diced red and orange/yellow bell peppers, cherry tomatoes, finely chopped red onion, chopped cilantro, and diced avocado.

Make Dressing:

- In a small bowl, whisk together lime juice, extra-virgin olive oil, ground cumin, chili powder, salt, and pepper. If you like a bit of heat, you can add minced jalapeño pepper to the dressing.

Toss Salad:

- Pour the dressing over the black bean and corn mixture. Gently toss everything until well combined.

Chill (Optional):

- For the best flavor, refrigerate the black bean and corn salad for at least 30 minutes to allow the flavors to meld.

Serve:

- Before serving, give the salad a final toss. Adjust seasoning if necessary and serve chilled or at room temperature.

This black bean and corn salad is not only delicious but also versatile. It can be served as a side dish with grilled chicken or fish, as a topping for tacos, or as a dip with tortilla chips. Enjoy the vibrant colors and fresh flavors of this nutritious salad!

Balsamic Glazed Brussels Sprouts

Ingredients:

- 1 pound Brussels sprouts, trimmed and halved
- 2 tablespoons olive oil
- Salt and pepper to taste
- 2 tablespoons balsamic vinegar
- 1 tablespoon honey or maple syrup
- 2 cloves garlic, minced (optional)
- 1/4 cup grated Parmesan cheese (optional)
- Crushed red pepper flakes for a hint of heat (optional)
- Chopped fresh parsley for garnish (optional)

Instructions:

Preheat Oven:
- Preheat your oven to 400°F (200°C).

Prepare Brussels Sprouts:
- Trim the ends of the Brussels sprouts and cut them in half.

Toss with Olive Oil:
- In a large bowl, toss the halved Brussels sprouts with olive oil, salt, and pepper until they are well coated.

Roast Brussels Sprouts:
- Spread the Brussels sprouts in a single layer on a baking sheet. Roast in the preheated oven for about 20-25 minutes or until they are golden brown and crispy on the edges. Stir or shake the pan halfway through for even cooking.

Prepare Glaze:
- In a small saucepan, combine balsamic vinegar, honey or maple syrup, and minced garlic (if using). Simmer over low heat for about 5 minutes or until the glaze thickens slightly.

Glaze Brussels Sprouts:
- Drizzle the balsamic glaze over the roasted Brussels sprouts and toss to coat them evenly.

Optional Additions:
- Optionally, sprinkle with grated Parmesan cheese and crushed red pepper flakes for extra flavor and heat.

Garnish and Serve:

- Garnish the balsamic glazed Brussels sprouts with chopped fresh parsley and serve immediately.

This dish is a delicious way to enjoy Brussels sprouts, and the balsamic glaze adds a sweet and tangy flavor. It's a versatile side dish that can complement various meals. Enjoy your flavorful and caramelized balsamic glazed Brussels sprouts!

Tomato Basil Quinoa Stuffed Peppers

Ingredients:

- 4 large bell peppers, any color
- 1 cup quinoa, rinsed
- 2 cups vegetable broth or water
- 1 tablespoon olive oil
- 1 onion, finely chopped
- 2 cloves garlic, minced
- 1 can (14 ounces) diced tomatoes, drained
- 1 cup cherry tomatoes, halved
- 1/2 cup fresh basil, chopped
- 1 teaspoon dried oregano
- Salt and pepper to taste
- 1 cup shredded mozzarella or Parmesan cheese (optional)

Instructions:

Preheat Oven:
- Preheat your oven to 375°F (190°C).

Prepare Quinoa:
- In a medium saucepan, combine quinoa and vegetable broth or water. Bring to a boil, then reduce heat to low, cover, and simmer for about 15-20 minutes or until quinoa is cooked and liquid is absorbed. Fluff the quinoa with a fork and set aside.

Prepare Peppers:
- Cut the tops off the bell peppers and remove the seeds and membranes. If needed, trim the bottoms of the peppers to help them stand upright in the baking dish.

Sauté Onion and Garlic:
- In a skillet, heat olive oil over medium heat. Add chopped onion and minced garlic. Sauté until the onion is softened.

Combine Ingredients:
- In a large bowl, combine the cooked quinoa, sautéed onion and garlic, diced tomatoes, cherry tomatoes, chopped fresh basil, dried oregano, salt, and pepper. Mix well.

Stuff Peppers:
- Stuff each bell pepper with the quinoa mixture, pressing it down gently.

Optional Cheese Topping:
- If desired, sprinkle shredded mozzarella or Parmesan cheese on top of each stuffed pepper.

Bake:
- Place the stuffed peppers in a baking dish. Bake in the preheated oven for about 25-30 minutes or until the peppers are tender.

Serve:
- Remove from the oven and let the stuffed peppers cool for a few minutes before serving.

These Tomato Basil Quinoa Stuffed Peppers are a delicious and well-balanced meal. You can customize the recipe by adding your favorite vegetables or protein. Enjoy this wholesome and flavorful dish!

Greek Yogurt Parfait with Berries

Ingredients:

- 1 cup Greek yogurt (plain or flavored)
- 1 cup mixed berries (strawberries, blueberries, raspberries)
- 1/4 cup granola
- 1 tablespoon honey or maple syrup (optional)
- Fresh mint leaves for garnish (optional)

Instructions:

Prepare Berries:
- Wash and dry the berries. If using strawberries, hull and slice them.

Layer Yogurt and Berries:
- In a glass or a bowl, start by layering a spoonful of Greek yogurt at the bottom.
- Add a layer of mixed berries on top of the yogurt.
- Repeat the layers until you reach the top, finishing with a layer of berries.

Top with Granola:
- Sprinkle granola on the top layer of berries for a crunchy texture.

Drizzle with Honey (Optional):
- If you like added sweetness, drizzle honey or maple syrup over the parfait.

Garnish (Optional):
- Garnish with fresh mint leaves for a burst of freshness and a pop of color.

Serve:
- Serve the Greek Yogurt Parfait with Berries immediately and enjoy!

This parfait is not only delicious but also versatile. You can customize it by adding nuts, seeds, or a dollop of nut butter for extra flavor and texture. It's a perfect breakfast, snack, or even a healthy dessert option. Enjoy the goodness of Greek yogurt and the natural sweetness of fresh berries!

Turkey and Vegetable Skillet

Ingredients:

- 1 pound ground turkey
- 1 tablespoon olive oil
- 1 onion, diced
- 2 bell peppers, diced (any color)
- 2 zucchini, diced
- 2 cloves garlic, minced
- 1 teaspoon dried oregano
- 1 teaspoon ground cumin
- 1 teaspoon paprika
- Salt and pepper to taste
- 1 can (14 ounces) diced tomatoes, undrained
- 1 cup cooked quinoa or rice
- Fresh parsley or cilantro for garnish (optional)

Instructions:

Cook Ground Turkey:
- In a large skillet, heat olive oil over medium heat. Add ground turkey and cook until browned, breaking it apart with a spoon as it cooks.

Add Aromatics:
- Add diced onion and minced garlic to the skillet. Sauté for a few minutes until the onion is softened.

Add Vegetables:
- Add diced bell peppers and zucchini to the skillet. Cook for about 5-7 minutes or until the vegetables are tender.

Season:
- Season the mixture with dried oregano, ground cumin, paprika, salt, and pepper. Stir well to combine.

Add Diced Tomatoes:
- Pour in the can of diced tomatoes with their juices. Stir and let the mixture simmer for 5-7 minutes.

Combine with Quinoa or Rice:
- Add cooked quinoa or rice to the skillet. Stir to combine and let it cook for an additional 2-3 minutes to heat through.

Adjust Seasoning:

- Taste and adjust the seasoning if needed. Add more salt, pepper, or spices according to your preference.

Garnish and Serve:
- Garnish with fresh parsley or cilantro if desired. Serve the Turkey and Vegetable Skillet hot.

This Turkey and Vegetable Skillet is a balanced and flavorful dish that provides protein and a variety of veggies. It's a versatile recipe, and you can customize it by adding your favorite vegetables or herbs. Enjoy this quick and wholesome meal!

Roasted Eggplant Dip (Baba Ganoush)

Ingredients:

- 2 medium-sized eggplants
- 2 cloves garlic, minced
- 2 tablespoons tahini (sesame paste)
- 3 tablespoons lemon juice
- 2 tablespoons extra-virgin olive oil
- 1/2 teaspoon ground cumin
- Salt and pepper to taste
- Fresh parsley for garnish
- Optional: Smoked paprika for garnish

Instructions:

Roast Eggplants:
- Preheat the oven to 400°F (200°C). Pierce the eggplants with a fork and place them on a baking sheet. Roast in the oven for about 40-45 minutes or until the skin is charred, and the eggplants are soft. You can also roast them on an open flame on a gas stove if you prefer.

Cool and Peel:
- Allow the roasted eggplants to cool slightly. Once cooled, peel off the charred skin, and discard it. Place the flesh in a bowl.

Mash Eggplant:
- Mash the roasted eggplant flesh with a fork or potato masher. You can leave it a bit chunky for texture.

Add Ingredients:
- Add minced garlic, tahini, lemon juice, extra-virgin olive oil, ground cumin, salt, and pepper to the mashed eggplant.

Blend or Mix:
- You can use a food processor to blend the ingredients until smooth or simply mix them well with a spoon for a chunkier texture.

Adjust Seasoning:
- Taste the baba ganoush and adjust the seasoning if needed. Add more salt, lemon juice, or olive oil according to your preference.

Chill (Optional):
- For enhanced flavor, refrigerate the baba ganoush for at least 1 hour before serving.

Garnish and Serve:
- Before serving, garnish with chopped fresh parsley and a sprinkle of smoked paprika if desired.

Serve with Pita or Vegetables:
- Serve the Roasted Eggplant Dip (Baba Ganoush) with pita bread, pita chips, or fresh vegetable sticks.

Enjoy this creamy and smoky dip as an appetizer or snack. Baba Ganoush is a crowd-pleaser and a great addition to your mezze platter.

Cilantro Lime Shrimp Lettuce Wraps

Ingredients:

For the Cilantro Lime Shrimp:

- 1 pound large shrimp, peeled and deveined
- 2 tablespoons olive oil
- 3 cloves garlic, minced
- Zest and juice of 2 limes
- 2 tablespoons fresh cilantro, chopped
- 1 teaspoon ground cumin
- Salt and pepper to taste
- Red pepper flakes for a hint of heat (optional)

For the Lettuce Wraps:

- Iceberg or butter lettuce leaves, washed and separated
- Avocado slices
- Cherry tomatoes, halved
- Red onion, thinly sliced
- Additional fresh cilantro for garnish
- Lime wedges for serving

Instructions:

Marinate Shrimp:
- In a bowl, combine shrimp with olive oil, minced garlic, lime zest, lime juice, chopped cilantro, ground cumin, salt, pepper, and red pepper flakes (if using). Allow the shrimp to marinate for about 15-20 minutes.

Cook Shrimp:
- Heat a skillet over medium-high heat. Add the marinated shrimp to the skillet and cook for 2-3 minutes per side or until the shrimp are opaque and cooked through.

Assemble Lettuce Wraps:
- Place a few cooked shrimp in each lettuce leaf.

Add Toppings:

- Top the shrimp with avocado slices, cherry tomato halves, and thinly sliced red onion.

Garnish:
- Garnish the lettuce wraps with additional fresh cilantro.

Serve:
- Serve the Cilantro Lime Shrimp Lettuce Wraps with lime wedges on the side.

These lettuce wraps are not only delicious but also a healthy and low-carb option. They make for a refreshing appetizer or a light meal. Feel free to customize the toppings with your favorite vegetables or add a dollop of Greek yogurt or salsa for extra flavor. Enjoy the vibrant and zesty Cilantro Lime Shrimp Lettuce Wraps!

Spaghetti Squash with Tomato Sauce

Ingredients:

- 1 medium-sized spaghetti squash
- 2 tablespoons olive oil
- 1 onion, finely chopped
- 2 cloves garlic, minced
- 1 can (14 ounces) crushed tomatoes
- 1 teaspoon dried oregano
- 1 teaspoon dried basil
- Salt and pepper to taste
- Grated Parmesan cheese for serving (optional)
- Fresh basil or parsley for garnish (optional)

Instructions:

Prepare Spaghetti Squash:
- Preheat the oven to 400°F (200°C). Cut the spaghetti squash in half lengthwise and scoop out the seeds. Drizzle the cut sides with olive oil and season with salt and pepper.

Roast Spaghetti Squash:
- Place the squash halves, cut side down, on a baking sheet. Roast in the preheated oven for 40-50 minutes or until the squash is tender and easily pierced with a fork.

Scrape Squash into "Noodles":
- Let the roasted spaghetti squash cool for a few minutes. Using a fork, scrape the flesh of the squash into strands, creating "noodles." Place the noodles in a large bowl.

Prepare Tomato Sauce:
- In a saucepan, heat olive oil over medium heat. Add finely chopped onion and minced garlic. Sauté until the onion is softened.

Add Crushed Tomatoes and Seasonings:
- Pour in the crushed tomatoes, dried oregano, dried basil, salt, and pepper. Stir well and bring the sauce to a simmer. Let it simmer for 15-20 minutes to allow the flavors to meld.

Combine with Spaghetti Squash:
- Pour the tomato sauce over the spaghetti squash noodles. Toss until the noodles are evenly coated with the sauce.

Serve:
- Serve the spaghetti squash with tomato sauce hot. Optionally, garnish with grated Parmesan cheese and fresh basil or parsley.

This Spaghetti Squash with Tomato Sauce is a healthy and satisfying dish that mimics the texture of traditional pasta while providing a nutrient-packed alternative. Customize it with your favorite herbs, spices, or additional vegetables. Enjoy your flavorful and guilt-free spaghetti squash meal!

Mushroom and Spinach Stuffed Chicken Breast

Ingredients:

- 4 boneless, skinless chicken breasts
- Salt and pepper to taste
- 1 tablespoon olive oil
- 2 cups baby spinach, chopped
- 2 cups mushrooms, finely chopped
- 2 cloves garlic, minced
- 1/2 cup shredded mozzarella or feta cheese
- 1 teaspoon dried thyme
- 1 teaspoon dried rosemary
- 1/2 cup chicken broth
- 1 tablespoon butter
- Fresh parsley for garnish (optional)

Instructions:

Preheat Oven:
- Preheat your oven to 375°F (190°C).

Prepare Chicken Breasts:
- Season the chicken breasts with salt and pepper. Carefully cut a slit along the side of each chicken breast to create a pocket for the stuffing.

Sauté Spinach and Mushrooms:
- In a skillet, heat olive oil over medium heat. Add chopped spinach, mushrooms, and minced garlic. Sauté until the vegetables are softened and any excess liquid has evaporated.

Add Cheese and Herbs:
- Stir in the shredded mozzarella or feta cheese, dried thyme, and dried rosemary. Mix until the cheese is melted and the stuffing is well combined.

Stuff Chicken Breasts:
- Stuff each chicken breast with the mushroom and spinach mixture, pressing the edges to seal.

Brown Chicken:
- In the same skillet, sear the stuffed chicken breasts for 2-3 minutes on each side or until golden brown.

Transfer to Oven:

- Transfer the chicken breasts to a baking dish. Pour chicken broth into the dish and place a small piece of butter on top of each stuffed chicken breast.

Bake:
- Bake in the preheated oven for 20-25 minutes or until the chicken is cooked through.

Garnish and Serve:
- Garnish with fresh parsley if desired. Serve the mushroom and spinach stuffed chicken breasts hot.

This dish is not only visually appealing but also rich in flavors. The combination of mushrooms, spinach, and cheese creates a delicious filling for the chicken. Enjoy your delightful and savory stuffed chicken breast!

Sweet Potato and Kale Hash

Ingredients:

- 2 medium-sized sweet potatoes, peeled and diced
- 1 bunch of kale, stems removed and leaves chopped
- 1 onion, finely chopped
- 2 cloves garlic, minced
- 2 tablespoons olive oil
- 1 teaspoon smoked paprika
- 1/2 teaspoon ground cumin
- Salt and pepper to taste
- Poached or fried eggs for serving (optional)

Instructions:

Prepare Sweet Potatoes:
- Peel the sweet potatoes and dice them into small cubes.

Sauté Onions and Garlic:
- In a large skillet, heat olive oil over medium heat. Add finely chopped onions and minced garlic. Sauté until the onions are translucent.

Add Sweet Potatoes:
- Add the diced sweet potatoes to the skillet. Cook for about 10-15 minutes or until the sweet potatoes are tender, stirring occasionally.

Season with Spices:
- Sprinkle smoked paprika, ground cumin, salt, and pepper over the sweet potatoes. Stir to coat the sweet potatoes with the spices.

Add Kale:
- Add the chopped kale to the skillet. Cook for an additional 5-7 minutes or until the kale is wilted and tender.

Adjust Seasoning:
- Taste the sweet potato and kale hash and adjust the seasoning if needed. Add more salt, pepper, or spices according to your preference.

Serve:
- Optionally, top the sweet potato and kale hash with poached or fried eggs for added protein.

Enjoy:
- Serve the sweet potato and kale hash hot and enjoy a delicious and nutritious meal!

This sweet potato and kale hash is a versatile dish that can be enjoyed on its own or as a side. It's a great way to incorporate colorful vegetables into your diet. Customize the recipe by adding your favorite herbs or spices. Enjoy the delightful combination of sweet potatoes and hearty kale!

Tuna and White Bean Salad

Ingredients:

- 2 cans (15 ounces each) white beans (cannellini or Great Northern), drained and rinsed
- 2 cans (5 ounces each) tuna, drained
- 1/2 red onion, finely chopped
- 1/2 cup cherry tomatoes, halved
- 1/4 cup Kalamata olives, sliced
- 1/4 cup fresh parsley, chopped
- 1/4 cup extra-virgin olive oil
- 2 tablespoons red wine vinegar
- 1 teaspoon Dijon mustard
- Salt and pepper to taste
- Optional: Feta cheese for garnish

Instructions:

Prepare White Beans and Tuna:
- In a large bowl, combine the drained and rinsed white beans with the drained tuna.

Add Vegetables:
- Add finely chopped red onion, cherry tomatoes, sliced Kalamata olives, and chopped fresh parsley to the bowl.

Make Dressing:
- In a small bowl, whisk together extra-virgin olive oil, red wine vinegar, Dijon mustard, salt, and pepper to create the dressing.

Combine and Toss:
- Pour the dressing over the white bean and tuna mixture. Gently toss everything together until well combined.

Adjust Seasoning:
- Taste the salad and adjust the seasoning if needed. Add more salt, pepper, or a splash of vinegar according to your preference.

Optional: Garnish with Feta:
- If desired, crumble feta cheese over the top of the salad for an extra burst of flavor.

Chill (Optional):

- For enhanced flavors, refrigerate the tuna and white bean salad for at least 30 minutes before serving.

Serve:
- Serve the tuna and white bean salad as a refreshing and protein-rich dish.

This tuna and white bean salad is versatile and can be served on its own, on a bed of greens, or in a sandwich. It's a great option for a quick and healthy lunch or dinner. Enjoy the combination of tuna, white beans, and vibrant Mediterranean flavors!

Cabbage and Apple Slaw

Ingredients:

- 4 cups green cabbage, thinly sliced
- 2 medium-sized apples, cored and julienned
- 1/2 cup carrots, grated
- 1/4 cup red onion, finely sliced
- 1/4 cup fresh parsley, chopped
- 1/4 cup mayonnaise
- 2 tablespoons apple cider vinegar
- 1 tablespoon Dijon mustard
- 1 tablespoon honey or maple syrup
- Salt and pepper to taste
- Optional: Chopped nuts (walnuts or pecans) for garnish

Instructions:

Prepare Vegetables and Apples:
- Thinly slice the green cabbage, julienne the apples, grate the carrots, finely slice the red onion, and chop the fresh parsley.

Combine Vegetables and Apples:
- In a large bowl, combine the sliced cabbage, julienned apples, grated carrots, sliced red onion, and chopped parsley.

Make Dressing:
- In a small bowl, whisk together mayonnaise, apple cider vinegar, Dijon mustard, honey or maple syrup, salt, and pepper to create the dressing.

Toss with Dressing:
- Pour the dressing over the cabbage and apple mixture. Toss everything together until the slaw is well coated with the dressing.

Chill (Optional):
- For enhanced flavors, refrigerate the cabbage and apple slaw for at least 30 minutes before serving.

Garnish (Optional):
- Optionally, garnish the slaw with chopped nuts (walnuts or pecans) for added texture and flavor.

Serve:

- Serve the cabbage and apple slaw as a refreshing side dish. It's great for picnics, barbecues, or as a topping for sandwiches.

This cabbage and apple slaw is a delightful combination of sweet and savory flavors, making it a perfect accompaniment to various dishes. Enjoy the crisp and crunchy texture along with the natural sweetness of apples!

Grilled Veggie and Hummus Wrap

Ingredients:

For the Grilled Veggies:

- 1 zucchini, sliced
- 1 yellow bell pepper, sliced
- 1 red onion, sliced
- 1 cup cherry tomatoes, halved
- 2 tablespoons olive oil
- Salt and pepper to taste
- 1 teaspoon dried oregano
- 1 teaspoon smoked paprika (optional)

For the Wrap:

- Whole wheat or spinach tortillas
- Hummus (store-bought or homemade)
- Fresh spinach leaves
- Feta cheese, crumbled (optional)
- Kalamata olives, sliced (optional)
- Fresh basil or cilantro leaves for garnish (optional)

Instructions:

Prepare Grilled Veggies:
- In a bowl, toss the sliced zucchini, yellow bell pepper, red onion, and cherry tomatoes with olive oil, salt, pepper, dried oregano, and smoked paprika (if using).

Grill Veggies:
- Heat a grill pan or grill over medium-high heat. Grill the veggies for about 5-7 minutes or until they are tender and have grill marks. Alternatively, you can roast them in the oven.

Assemble Wrap:
- Lay out the whole wheat or spinach tortillas. Spread a generous layer of hummus over each tortilla.

Add Grilled Veggies:
- Place a portion of the grilled veggies on top of the hummus.

Add Spinach and Optional Toppings:
- Add fresh spinach leaves on top of the veggies. Optionally, sprinkle crumbled feta cheese and sliced Kalamata olives for extra flavor.

Garnish:
- Garnish the wrap with fresh basil or cilantro leaves.

Fold and Serve:
- Fold the sides of the tortilla and roll it up to create the wrap.

Slice (Optional):
- Optionally, slice the wraps in half diagonally for easier handling.

Serve:
- Serve the grilled veggie and hummus wraps immediately. They can be enjoyed warm or at room temperature.

These wraps are not only tasty but also versatile. Feel free to customize them with your favorite veggies, herbs, or additional toppings. Enjoy a healthy and flavorful meal with this grilled veggie and hummus wrap!

Sesame Soy Marinated Tofu

Ingredients:

- 1 block extra-firm tofu, pressed and cut into cubes
- 2 tablespoons soy sauce
- 1 tablespoon sesame oil
- 1 tablespoon rice vinegar
- 1 tablespoon maple syrup or agave nectar
- 2 cloves garlic, minced
- 1 teaspoon grated ginger
- 1 tablespoon sesame seeds (white or black)
- Green onions, chopped, for garnish (optional)

Instructions:

Press Tofu:
- Press the tofu to remove excess water. You can do this by placing the block of tofu between two plates and putting something heavy on top. Let it press for at least 15-20 minutes.

Prepare Marinade:
- In a bowl, whisk together soy sauce, sesame oil, rice vinegar, maple syrup or agave nectar, minced garlic, and grated ginger.

Marinate Tofu:
- Cut the pressed tofu into cubes and place them in a shallow dish or a zip-top bag. Pour the marinade over the tofu, making sure each piece is well coated. Let it marinate for at least 30 minutes to allow the flavors to absorb.

Cook Tofu:
- Heat a skillet or grill pan over medium-high heat. Add the marinated tofu cubes, reserving the marinade. Cook the tofu for 3-5 minutes on each side or until golden and slightly crispy.

Simmer Marinade (Optional):
- If desired, you can simmer the reserved marinade in a small saucepan for a few minutes until it thickens slightly. Use this as a drizzle or dipping sauce.

Garnish and Serve:

- Garnish the sesame soy marinated tofu with sesame seeds and chopped green onions. Serve it over rice, quinoa, or your favorite grains.

This sesame soy marinated tofu is a delicious and protein-packed option that can be enjoyed as a main course, added to salads, or used in wraps. It's a versatile dish with a perfect balance of savory and sweet flavors. Feel free to customize the marinade to suit your taste preferences. Enjoy your sesame soy marinated tofu!

Mediterranean Quinoa Bowl

Ingredients:

For the Quinoa:

- 1 cup quinoa, rinsed
- 2 cups vegetable broth or water
- 1 tablespoon olive oil
- Salt to taste

For the Bowl:

- 1 cup cherry tomatoes, halved
- 1 cucumber, diced
- 1/2 cup Kalamata olives, sliced
- 1/2 cup red onion, finely chopped
- 1/2 cup feta cheese, crumbled
- 1/4 cup fresh parsley, chopped
- 1/4 cup fresh mint, chopped

For the Dressing:

- 1/4 cup extra-virgin olive oil
- 2 tablespoons red wine vinegar
- 1 clove garlic, minced
- 1 teaspoon dried oregano
- Salt and pepper to taste

Instructions:

Prepare Quinoa:
- In a medium saucepan, combine quinoa and vegetable broth or water. Bring to a boil, then reduce heat to low, cover, and simmer for about 15-20 minutes or until quinoa is cooked and liquid is absorbed. Fluff the quinoa with a fork and let it cool.

Make Dressing:
- In a small bowl, whisk together olive oil, red wine vinegar, minced garlic, dried oregano, salt, and pepper to create the dressing.

Assemble Bowl:

- In a large bowl, combine cooked quinoa, cherry tomatoes, diced cucumber, Kalamata olives, chopped red onion, crumbled feta cheese, fresh parsley, and fresh mint.

Pour Dressing:
- Pour the dressing over the quinoa and vegetable mixture. Toss everything together until well combined.

Adjust Seasoning:
- Taste the Mediterranean quinoa bowl and adjust the seasoning if needed. Add more salt, pepper, or a splash of red wine vinegar according to your preference.

Serve:
- Divide the Mediterranean quinoa bowl into serving bowls. Optionally, garnish with additional fresh herbs.

This Mediterranean quinoa bowl is a complete and satisfying meal on its own. It's packed with a variety of textures and flavors from fresh vegetables, herbs, and feta cheese. Enjoy this wholesome and delicious dish as a light lunch or dinner!

Stir-Fried Brown Rice with Vegetables

Ingredients:

- 2 cups cooked brown rice (preferably cooled or day-old)
- 2 tablespoons vegetable oil
- 1 onion, finely chopped
- 2 carrots, julienned
- 1 bell pepper (any color), thinly sliced
- 1 zucchini, diced
- 1 cup broccoli florets
- 2 cloves garlic, minced
- 1 tablespoon ginger, minced
- 3 tablespoons soy sauce
- 1 tablespoon oyster sauce (optional)
- 1 teaspoon sesame oil
- 2 green onions, sliced (for garnish)
- Sesame seeds (for garnish, optional)

Instructions:

Prepare Ingredients:
- If you haven't cooked the brown rice yet, cook it according to package instructions and let it cool. Having cooled or day-old rice works best for stir-frying.

Heat Oil:
- Heat vegetable oil in a large wok or skillet over medium-high heat.

Sauté Aromatics:
- Add finely chopped onion, minced garlic, and minced ginger to the hot oil. Sauté for 1-2 minutes until fragrant.

Add Vegetables:
- Add julienned carrots, sliced bell pepper, diced zucchini, and broccoli florets to the wok. Stir-fry the vegetables for about 5-7 minutes or until they are slightly tender but still crisp.

Add Rice:
- Add the cooked brown rice to the wok. Break up any clumps and toss the rice with the vegetables.

Season:

- Pour soy sauce, oyster sauce (if using), and sesame oil over the rice and vegetables. Stir well to ensure even distribution of the sauces.

Stir-Fry:
- Continue to stir-fry the brown rice and vegetables for an additional 5-7 minutes, allowing the flavors to meld and the rice to get slightly crispy.

Adjust Seasoning:
- Taste and adjust the seasoning if needed. You can add more soy sauce or a dash of salt and pepper according to your preference.

Garnish and Serve:
- Garnish the stir-fried brown rice with sliced green onions and sesame seeds if desired.

Serve Hot:
- Serve the stir-fried brown rice with vegetables hot as a delicious and wholesome meal.

This stir-fried brown rice with vegetables is not only tasty but also a great way to incorporate a variety of colorful vegetables into your diet. Feel free to customize the vegetables and adjust the seasoning to suit your taste. Enjoy this simple and nutritious dish!

Lemon Herb Tilapia

Ingredients:

- 4 tilapia fillets
- 2 tablespoons olive oil
- 2 tablespoons fresh lemon juice
- 2 cloves garlic, minced
- 1 teaspoon dried oregano
- 1 teaspoon dried thyme
- 1 teaspoon paprika
- Salt and pepper to taste
- Lemon slices for garnish
- Fresh parsley, chopped, for garnish

Instructions:

Preheat Oven:
- Preheat your oven to 400°F (200°C).

Prepare Tilapia Fillets:
- Pat the tilapia fillets dry with paper towels. Place them on a baking sheet lined with parchment paper or lightly greased.

Make Marinade:
- In a small bowl, whisk together olive oil, fresh lemon juice, minced garlic, dried oregano, dried thyme, paprika, salt, and pepper to create the marinade.

Marinate Tilapia:
- Brush the tilapia fillets with the lemon herb marinade, ensuring they are well coated on both sides.

Bake:
- Bake the tilapia in the preheated oven for about 12-15 minutes or until the fish is cooked through and easily flakes with a fork.

Broil (Optional):
- If you prefer a slightly crispy top, you can broil the tilapia for an additional 2-3 minutes at the end.

Garnish:
- Garnish the lemon herb tilapia with lemon slices and chopped fresh parsley.

Serve:

- Serve the tilapia fillets hot, either on their own or with your favorite side dishes.

This lemon herb tilapia is a simple and healthy option for a quick weeknight dinner. The combination of citrusy lemon and aromatic herbs adds brightness and depth of flavor to the mild tilapia. Enjoy this delicious and light seafood dish!

Cauliflower Mashed Potatoes

Ingredients:

- 1 medium-sized cauliflower head, chopped into florets
- 2 tablespoons butter
- 2 cloves garlic, minced
- 1/4 cup grated Parmesan cheese
- Salt and pepper to taste
- Chopped fresh chives or parsley for garnish (optional)

Instructions:

Steam Cauliflower:
- Place the cauliflower florets in a steamer basket over a pot of boiling water. Steam for about 10-15 minutes or until the cauliflower is tender when pierced with a fork.

Drain and Dry:
- Drain the steamed cauliflower well to remove excess moisture. You can pat it dry with paper towels for better texture.

Mash Cauliflower:
- In a food processor or using a potato masher, process the steamed cauliflower until it reaches a mashed potato-like consistency. If using a food processor, pulse the cauliflower to avoid over-processing.

Sauté Garlic:
- In a skillet, melt butter over medium heat. Add minced garlic and sauté for 1-2 minutes until fragrant.

Combine with Cauliflower:
- Add the mashed cauliflower to the skillet with the sautéed garlic and butter. Mix well to combine.

Add Parmesan:
- Stir in grated Parmesan cheese, salt, and pepper. Continue to mix until the cheese is melted and the ingredients are well incorporated.

Adjust Seasoning:
- Taste the cauliflower mashed potatoes and adjust the seasoning if needed. Add more salt and pepper according to your preference.

Garnish:
- Optionally, garnish the cauliflower mashed potatoes with chopped fresh chives or parsley for added freshness and color.

Serve:
- Serve the cauliflower mashed potatoes hot as a side dish. They pair well with a variety of main courses.

This cauliflower mashed potatoes recipe is a healthier alternative that doesn't sacrifice flavor. It's a great option for those looking to reduce their carbohydrate intake or incorporate more vegetables into their meals. Enjoy the creamy and delicious cauliflower mashed potatoes!

Bruschetta Chicken

Ingredients:

For the Bruschetta Topping:

- 1 cup cherry tomatoes, diced
- 1/4 cup red onion, finely chopped
- 2 cloves garlic, minced
- 1/4 cup fresh basil, chopped
- 1 tablespoon balsamic vinegar
- 2 tablespoons extra-virgin olive oil
- Salt and pepper to taste

For the Chicken:

- 4 boneless, skinless chicken breasts
- Salt and pepper to taste
- 1 teaspoon dried oregano
- 1 teaspoon dried basil
- 1 tablespoon olive oil

Instructions:

Preheat Oven:
- Preheat your oven to 400°F (200°C).

Prepare Bruschetta Topping:
- In a bowl, combine diced cherry tomatoes, chopped red onion, minced garlic, chopped fresh basil, balsamic vinegar, extra-virgin olive oil, salt, and pepper. Mix well and set aside to let the flavors meld.

Season Chicken:
- Season the chicken breasts with salt, pepper, dried oregano, and dried basil on both sides.

Sear Chicken:
- Heat olive oil in an oven-safe skillet over medium-high heat. Sear the seasoned chicken breasts for 2-3 minutes on each side until they develop a golden brown crust.

Top with Bruschetta Mixture:
- Spoon the prepared bruschetta topping over each chicken breast in the skillet.

Bake:
- Transfer the skillet to the preheated oven and bake for 20-25 minutes or until the chicken is cooked through (with an internal temperature of 165°F or 74°C).

Serve:
- Remove the skillet from the oven and let it rest for a few minutes. Serve the bruschetta chicken hot, spooning the flavorful tomato and basil mixture over the chicken.

Garnish (Optional):
- Optionally, garnish with additional fresh basil before serving.

This bruschetta chicken is a perfect combination of juicy, seasoned chicken and the bright, fresh flavors of the tomato and basil topping. It's a delightful and easy-to-make dish that's sure to impress. Enjoy your bruschetta chicken with your favorite side dishes!

Kale and White Bean Soup

Ingredients:

- 1 tablespoon olive oil
- 1 onion, chopped
- 2 carrots, diced
- 2 celery stalks, diced
- 3 cloves garlic, minced
- 1 teaspoon dried thyme
- 1 teaspoon dried rosemary
- 1 bay leaf
- 4 cups vegetable or chicken broth
- 2 cans (15 ounces each) white beans (cannellini or Great Northern), drained and rinsed
- 1 bunch kale, stems removed and leaves chopped
- Salt and pepper to taste
- 1 tablespoon lemon juice (optional)
- Grated Parmesan cheese for serving (optional)

Instructions:

Sauté Vegetables:
- In a large pot, heat olive oil over medium heat. Add chopped onion, diced carrots, and diced celery. Sauté for about 5 minutes until the vegetables are softened.

Add Garlic and Herbs:
- Add minced garlic, dried thyme, dried rosemary, and bay leaf. Sauté for an additional 1-2 minutes until the garlic is fragrant.

Pour Broth:
- Pour in the vegetable or chicken broth. Bring the mixture to a simmer.

Add White Beans:
- Add the drained and rinsed white beans to the pot. Stir well.

Simmer:
- Let the soup simmer for about 15-20 minutes to allow the flavors to meld.

Add Kale:
- Add the chopped kale to the soup. Simmer for an additional 5-7 minutes or until the kale is tender.

Season:
- Season the soup with salt and pepper to taste. If desired, add lemon juice for a hint of brightness.

Serve:
- Remove the bay leaf and discard it. Ladle the kale and white bean soup into bowls.

Garnish (Optional):
- Optionally, garnish each serving with grated Parmesan cheese.

Enjoy:
- Serve the kale and white bean soup hot and enjoy a comforting and nutritious meal!

This kale and white bean soup is not only delicious but also packed with fiber and vitamins. It's a versatile recipe, and you can customize it by adding other vegetables or herbs according to your taste. Enjoy this wholesome and satisfying soup!

Avocado and Chickpea Salad

Ingredients:

- 1 can (15 ounces) chickpeas, drained and rinsed
- 2 ripe avocados, diced
- 1 cup cherry tomatoes, halved
- 1/4 cup red onion, finely chopped
- 1/4 cup fresh cilantro or parsley, chopped
- 1 clove garlic, minced
- 2 tablespoons extra-virgin olive oil
- 1 tablespoon red wine vinegar or lime juice
- Salt and pepper to taste
- Optional: Feta cheese for garnish

Instructions:

Prepare Chickpeas:
- In a bowl, combine the drained and rinsed chickpeas.

Dice Avocados:
- Dice the ripe avocados and add them to the bowl with chickpeas.

Add Vegetables:
- Add cherry tomatoes, finely chopped red onion, and chopped cilantro or parsley to the bowl.

Make Dressing:
- In a small bowl, whisk together minced garlic, extra-virgin olive oil, red wine vinegar or lime juice, salt, and pepper to create the dressing.

Combine and Toss:
- Pour the dressing over the chickpea and avocado mixture. Gently toss everything together until well combined.

Adjust Seasoning:
- Taste the salad and adjust the seasoning if needed. Add more salt, pepper, or a splash of vinegar according to your preference.

Optional: Garnish with Feta:
- If desired, crumble feta cheese over the top of the salad for added creaminess and flavor.

Chill (Optional):
- For enhanced flavors, refrigerate the avocado and chickpea salad for at least 30 minutes before serving.

Serve:
- Serve the avocado and chickpea salad as a refreshing and nutritious side dish or a light lunch.

This avocado and chickpea salad is a perfect combination of creamy avocados, protein-rich chickpeas, and fresh vegetables. It's a versatile recipe that can be customized with additional herbs, spices, or your favorite ingredients. Enjoy this healthy and delicious salad!

Salmon and Quinoa Patties

Ingredients:

- 1 cup cooked quinoa, cooled
- 2 cans (6 ounces each) canned salmon, drained and flaked
- 1/4 cup breadcrumbs
- 1/4 cup grated Parmesan cheese
- 1/4 cup red onion, finely chopped
- 2 cloves garlic, minced
- 1/4 cup fresh parsley, chopped
- 1 teaspoon Dijon mustard
- 1 large egg
- Zest and juice of 1 lemon
- Salt and pepper to taste
- Olive oil for cooking

Instructions:

Combine Ingredients:
- In a large bowl, combine cooked quinoa, canned salmon, breadcrumbs, grated Parmesan cheese, chopped red onion, minced garlic, chopped fresh parsley, Dijon mustard, egg, lemon zest, and lemon juice.

Season:
- Season the mixture with salt and pepper to taste. Mix all the ingredients until well combined.

Form Patties:
- Divide the mixture into equal portions and shape them into patties.

Chill (Optional):
- If time allows, refrigerate the patties for about 30 minutes. This helps them hold their shape better during cooking.

Cook Patties:
- Heat olive oil in a skillet over medium heat. Cook the salmon and quinoa patties for 3-4 minutes on each side or until they are golden brown and cooked through.

Serve:
- Serve the salmon and quinoa patties hot, either on their own or in a bun as a burger.

Optional Sauce:
- Consider serving with a side of Greek yogurt or tzatziki sauce for dipping.

Enjoy:
- Enjoy these flavorful and protein-packed salmon and quinoa patties!

These patties are not only delicious but also a great way to incorporate omega-3 rich salmon and quinoa into your diet. Customize the recipe with your favorite herbs and spices to suit your taste. Whether served as a main dish or in a bun as a burger, these patties are a wholesome and satisfying option.

Broccoli and Cauliflower Gratin

Ingredients:

- 1 head broccoli, cut into florets
- 1 head cauliflower, cut into florets
- 3 tablespoons butter
- 3 tablespoons all-purpose flour
- 2 cups milk
- 1 cup shredded cheddar cheese
- 1/2 cup grated Parmesan cheese
- Salt and pepper to taste
- 1/2 teaspoon nutmeg (optional)
- 1 cup breadcrumbs
- Chopped fresh parsley for garnish (optional)

Instructions:

Preheat Oven:
- Preheat your oven to 375°F (190°C).

Blanch Vegetables:
- Bring a large pot of salted water to a boil. Blanch the broccoli and cauliflower florets for about 3 minutes, then drain and set aside.

Make Cheese Sauce:
- In a saucepan, melt butter over medium heat. Add flour and stir to create a roux. Cook for 1-2 minutes, stirring constantly.

Add Milk:
- Gradually whisk in the milk to the roux, ensuring there are no lumps. Cook the mixture, stirring constantly, until it thickens.

Add Cheese:
- Stir in the shredded cheddar cheese and grated Parmesan cheese until melted and smooth. Season with salt, pepper, and nutmeg (if using).

Combine Vegetables and Cheese Sauce:
- Add the blanched broccoli and cauliflower florets to the cheese sauce. Gently toss until the vegetables are coated.

Transfer to Baking Dish:
- Transfer the mixture to a greased baking dish, spreading it evenly.

Prepare Topping:

- In a small bowl, combine breadcrumbs with a bit of melted butter. Sprinkle this breadcrumb mixture over the top of the vegetables.

Bake:
- Bake in the preheated oven for 25-30 minutes or until the top is golden brown and the vegetables are tender.

Garnish and Serve:
- Optionally, garnish with chopped fresh parsley before serving.

Enjoy:
- Serve the broccoli and cauliflower gratin hot as a delicious and comforting side dish.

This broccoli and cauliflower gratin is a crowd-pleaser with its creamy texture and cheesy topping. It's a perfect accompaniment to roasts, poultry, or as a standalone vegetarian dish. Enjoy this flavorful and comforting gratin!

Spicy Grilled Shrimp

Ingredients:

- 1 pound large shrimp, peeled and deveined
- 2 tablespoons olive oil
- 2 cloves garlic, minced
- 1 teaspoon smoked paprika
- 1 teaspoon cayenne pepper (adjust to taste for spiciness)
- 1 teaspoon cumin
- 1 teaspoon onion powder
- 1 teaspoon dried oregano
- Salt and black pepper to taste
- Fresh lemon wedges for serving

Instructions:

Preheat Grill:
- Preheat your grill to medium-high heat.

Marinate Shrimp:
- In a bowl, combine olive oil, minced garlic, smoked paprika, cayenne pepper, cumin, onion powder, dried oregano, salt, and black pepper. Mix well to create the marinade.

Coat Shrimp:
- Add the peeled and deveined shrimp to the marinade. Toss the shrimp until they are well coated with the spicy mixture. Allow them to marinate for about 15-30 minutes.

Skewer Shrimp:
- If using wooden skewers, soak them in water for about 15 minutes to prevent burning. Thread the marinated shrimp onto skewers.

Grill Shrimp:
- Place the shrimp skewers on the preheated grill. Grill for 2-3 minutes per side or until the shrimp are opaque and cooked through.

Serve:
- Remove the shrimp skewers from the grill and transfer them to a serving plate. Squeeze fresh lemon juice over the grilled shrimp for an extra burst of flavor.

Garnish (Optional):

- Optionally, garnish with chopped fresh parsley or cilantro before serving.

Enjoy:
- Serve the spicy grilled shrimp hot as an appetizer or as part of a main course. They pair well with rice, salads, or grilled vegetables.

These spicy grilled shrimp are not only delicious but also easy to prepare. The combination of smoky paprika, cayenne, and other spices gives the shrimp a bold and flavorful kick. Adjust the level of spiciness according to your preference, and enjoy this quick and tasty grilled shrimp dish!

Caprese Salad

Ingredients:

- 4 large ripe tomatoes, sliced
- 1 pound fresh mozzarella cheese, sliced
- Fresh basil leaves
- Extra-virgin olive oil
- Balsamic glaze or balsamic reduction
- Salt and black pepper to taste

Instructions:

Prepare Tomatoes:
- Wash and slice the tomatoes into 1/4-inch thick slices.

Slice Mozzarella:
- Slice the fresh mozzarella cheese into similar-sized slices as the tomatoes.

Assemble Salad:
- Arrange the tomato and mozzarella slices alternately on a serving platter.

Add Basil Leaves:
- Tuck fresh basil leaves between the tomato and mozzarella slices. You can use whole leaves or chiffonade the basil (stack the leaves, roll them, and thinly slice).

Drizzle Olive Oil:
- Drizzle extra-virgin olive oil over the tomato and mozzarella slices.

Season:
- Sprinkle salt and black pepper to taste over the salad.

Balsamic Glaze:
- Drizzle balsamic glaze or balsamic reduction over the salad for a sweet and tangy finish.

Serve:
- Serve the Caprese salad immediately as a refreshing appetizer or side dish.

Enjoy:
- Enjoy the classic combination of tomatoes, fresh mozzarella, and basil in this simple and elegant Caprese salad!

Caprese salad is known for its simplicity and the quality of its ingredients. It's a perfect dish to showcase the flavors of ripe summer tomatoes and the creaminess of fresh mozzarella. Customize the salad with your favorite balsamic glaze or reduction, and savor the vibrant and delicious combination of flavors.

Chia Seed Pudding with Berries

Ingredients:

- 1/4 cup chia seeds
- 1 cup milk (dairy or plant-based)
- 1-2 tablespoons honey or maple syrup (adjust to taste)
- 1/2 teaspoon vanilla extract
- Mixed berries (strawberries, blueberries, raspberries) for topping

Instructions:

Combine Chia Seeds and Liquid:
- In a bowl or jar, combine chia seeds, milk, honey or maple syrup, and vanilla extract. Mix well to ensure the chia seeds are evenly distributed.

Stir and Rest:
- Stir the mixture again after a few minutes to prevent clumping. Let the chia seed pudding mixture rest for about 15 minutes.

Stir Again and Refrigerate:
- Give the mixture one more stir, cover the bowl or jar, and refrigerate for at least 2-3 hours or overnight. This allows the chia seeds to absorb the liquid and create a pudding-like consistency.

Check and Adjust:
- After the initial refrigeration period, check the chia seed pudding. If it's too thick, you can add a bit more milk and stir to reach your desired consistency. If it's not sweet enough, add more honey or maple syrup.

Serve with Berries:
- Before serving, top the chia seed pudding with mixed berries. You can arrange them on top or mix them into the pudding.

Optional Garnishes:
- Optionally, garnish with additional toppings like shredded coconut, chopped nuts, or a drizzle of honey.

Enjoy:
- Serve the chia seed pudding with berries as a healthy and satisfying dessert or breakfast.

Chia seed pudding is not only delicious but also packed with fiber, omega-3 fatty acids, and other nutrients. It's a versatile dish that you can customize with your favorite toppings and flavors. Enjoy this nutritious and delightful chia seed pudding with a burst of fresh berries!

Sesame Ginger Chicken Stir-Fry

Ingredients:

For the Marinade:

- 1 pound boneless, skinless chicken breasts, thinly sliced
- 2 tablespoons soy sauce
- 1 tablespoon sesame oil
- 1 tablespoon rice vinegar
- 1 tablespoon honey or maple syrup
- 1 tablespoon fresh ginger, minced
- 2 cloves garlic, minced

For the Stir-Fry:

- 2 tablespoons vegetable oil
- 1 bell pepper, thinly sliced
- 1 cup broccoli florets
- 1 carrot, julienned
- 1 cup snap peas, ends trimmed
- 2 green onions, sliced (for garnish)
- Sesame seeds (for garnish)

For the Sauce:

- 2 tablespoons soy sauce
- 1 tablespoon oyster sauce
- 1 tablespoon hoisin sauce
- 1 teaspoon cornstarch (optional, for thickening)

Instructions:

Marinate Chicken:
- In a bowl, combine the sliced chicken with soy sauce, sesame oil, rice vinegar, honey or maple syrup, minced ginger, and minced garlic. Let it marinate for at least 15-20 minutes.

Prepare Sauce:
- In a small bowl, whisk together soy sauce, oyster sauce, hoisin sauce, and cornstarch (if using). Set aside.

Heat Oil:
- Heat vegetable oil in a wok or large skillet over high heat.

Cook Chicken:
- Add the marinated chicken to the hot pan. Stir-fry for 3-4 minutes or until the chicken is cooked through and slightly browned. Remove the chicken from the pan and set it aside.

Stir-Fry Vegetables:
- In the same pan, add a bit more oil if needed. Add bell pepper, broccoli florets, julienned carrot, and snap peas. Stir-fry for about 3-4 minutes or until the vegetables are tender-crisp.

Combine Chicken and Vegetables:
- Return the cooked chicken to the pan with the vegetables. Pour the prepared sauce over the chicken and vegetables. Toss everything together until well coated and heated through.

Garnish:
- Garnish the sesame ginger chicken stir-fry with sliced green onions and sesame seeds.

Serve:
- Serve the stir-fry over rice or noodles and enjoy this flavorful and satisfying dish!

This sesame ginger chicken stir-fry is not only delicious but also customizable. Feel free to add your favorite vegetables or adjust the level of spiciness to suit your taste. Enjoy the combination of tender chicken, crisp vegetables, and the aromatic sesame ginger sauce!

Quinoa-Stuffed Bell Peppers

Ingredients:

- 4 large bell peppers, halved and seeds removed
- 1 cup quinoa, rinsed and cooked according to package instructions
- 1 tablespoon olive oil
- 1 onion, finely chopped
- 2 cloves garlic, minced
- 1 zucchini, diced
- 1 cup cherry tomatoes, halved
- 1 cup black beans, drained and rinsed
- 1 cup corn kernels (fresh, frozen, or canned)
- 1 teaspoon ground cumin
- 1 teaspoon chili powder
- Salt and pepper to taste
- 1 cup shredded cheese (cheddar, Monterey Jack, or a blend)
- Fresh cilantro or parsley for garnish (optional)
- Salsa or avocado for serving (optional)

Instructions:

Preheat Oven:
- Preheat your oven to 375°F (190°C).

Prepare Bell Peppers:
- Cut the bell peppers in half lengthwise and remove the seeds and membranes. Place the pepper halves in a baking dish.

Cook Quinoa:
- Cook the quinoa according to package instructions. Set aside.

Sauté Vegetables:
- In a large skillet, heat olive oil over medium heat. Add chopped onion and sauté until softened. Add minced garlic and cook for an additional 1-2 minutes.

Add Zucchini and Tomatoes:
- Add diced zucchini and halved cherry tomatoes to the skillet. Cook for 3-4 minutes until the vegetables are tender.

Combine Quinoa and Vegetables:

- In a large bowl, combine the cooked quinoa with the sautéed vegetables. Add black beans, corn, ground cumin, chili powder, salt, and pepper. Mix well.

Stuff Bell Peppers:
- Stuff each bell pepper half with the quinoa and vegetable mixture. Press down gently to pack the filling.

Top with Cheese:
- Sprinkle shredded cheese over the top of each stuffed pepper.

Bake:
- Bake in the preheated oven for 25-30 minutes or until the peppers are tender and the cheese is melted and bubbly.

Garnish and Serve:
- Garnish with fresh cilantro or parsley if desired. Serve the quinoa-stuffed bell peppers with salsa or sliced avocado on the side.

Enjoy:
- Enjoy these delicious and nutritious quinoa-stuffed bell peppers as a wholesome and satisfying meal!

This recipe is versatile, and you can customize the filling with your favorite vegetables and seasonings. The combination of quinoa, vegetables, and melted cheese makes for a tasty and well-balanced dish.

Eggplant and Tomato Bake

Ingredients:

- 2 large eggplants, sliced into 1/2-inch rounds
- 4 large tomatoes, sliced
- 1 onion, thinly sliced
- 3 cloves garlic, minced
- 1/4 cup fresh basil, chopped
- 1/4 cup fresh parsley, chopped
- 1 teaspoon dried oregano
- 1 teaspoon dried thyme
- Salt and black pepper to taste
- Olive oil for drizzling
- 1 cup shredded mozzarella cheese (optional)
- Grated Parmesan cheese for topping

Instructions:

Preheat Oven:
- Preheat your oven to 375°F (190°C).

Prepare Eggplants:
- Slice the eggplants into rounds, about 1/2-inch thick. Lay the slices on a baking sheet and sprinkle them with salt. Allow them to sit for about 15-20 minutes to release excess moisture. Pat the eggplant slices dry with paper towels.

Sauté Onion and Garlic:
- In a skillet, heat olive oil over medium heat. Add sliced onion and minced garlic. Sauté until the onion is translucent.

Layer Eggplants and Tomatoes:
- In a baking dish, layer the eggplant slices, tomato slices, sautéed onion and garlic, chopped basil, chopped parsley, dried oregano, and dried thyme. Repeat the layers until all ingredients are used.

Season:
- Season each layer with salt and black pepper to taste.

Drizzle Olive Oil:
- Drizzle olive oil over the top of the layers.

Optional Cheese Layer:

- If desired, sprinkle shredded mozzarella cheese over the top for an extra cheesy layer.

Bake:
- Cover the baking dish with foil and bake in the preheated oven for 25-30 minutes. Then, remove the foil and bake for an additional 10-15 minutes or until the vegetables are tender and the top is golden brown.

Broil (Optional):
- For a golden crust, you can broil the dish for a few minutes at the end.

Top with Parmesan:
- Sprinkle grated Parmesan cheese over the top before serving.

Serve:
- Serve the eggplant and tomato bake hot as a flavorful and satisfying side dish or main course.

Enjoy this eggplant and tomato bake as a comforting and hearty dish that showcases the wonderful flavors of fresh vegetables and herbs!

Roasted Red Pepper Hummus

Ingredients:

- 1 can (15 ounces) chickpeas, drained and rinsed
- 1/2 cup roasted red peppers (store-bought or homemade)
- 1/4 cup tahini
- 2 tablespoons extra-virgin olive oil, plus extra for drizzling
- 2 tablespoons freshly squeezed lemon juice
- 2 cloves garlic, minced
- 1/2 teaspoon ground cumin
- 1/2 teaspoon smoked paprika
- Salt and black pepper to taste
- Water (as needed to adjust consistency)

Optional Garnish:

- Chopped fresh parsley
- Additional roasted red peppers
- Drizzle of olive oil
- Pinch of smoked paprika

Instructions:

Prepare Roasted Red Peppers:
- If using homemade roasted red peppers, you can roast them in the oven or use jarred roasted red peppers. Drain any excess liquid.

Combine Ingredients:
- In a food processor, combine chickpeas, roasted red peppers, tahini, olive oil, lemon juice, minced garlic, ground cumin, smoked paprika, salt, and black pepper.

Process until Smooth:
- Process the ingredients until smooth and creamy. If the hummus is too thick, you can add water, a tablespoon at a time, until you reach your desired consistency.

Adjust Seasoning:
- Taste the hummus and adjust the seasoning as needed. Add more salt, pepper, or lemon juice to suit your taste.

Serve:
- Transfer the roasted red pepper hummus to a serving bowl.

Garnish (Optional):
- Garnish the hummus with chopped fresh parsley, additional roasted red peppers, a drizzle of olive oil, and a pinch of smoked paprika.

Enjoy:
- Serve the roasted red pepper hummus with pita bread, vegetable sticks, or as a spread for sandwiches and wraps.

This roasted red pepper hummus is a flavorful and vibrant dip that adds a unique twist to your snacking or appetizer spread. It's perfect for gatherings or as a tasty and healthy snack option. Enjoy the rich and smoky flavor of roasted red peppers in this delicious hummus!

Lemon Herb Roasted Vegetables

Ingredients:

- Assorted vegetables (such as carrots, bell peppers, zucchini, cherry tomatoes, and red onions), washed and chopped into bite-sized pieces
- 3 tablespoons olive oil
- 2 tablespoons fresh lemon juice
- 2 cloves garlic, minced
- 1 teaspoon dried thyme
- 1 teaspoon dried rosemary
- 1 teaspoon dried oregano
- Salt and black pepper to taste
- Zest of 1 lemon
- Fresh parsley for garnish (optional)

Instructions:

Preheat Oven:
- Preheat your oven to 400°F (200°C).

Prepare Vegetables:
- Wash and chop the assorted vegetables into bite-sized pieces. You can use a mix of carrots, bell peppers, zucchini, cherry tomatoes, and red onions, or any vegetables of your choice.

Prepare Lemon Herb Marinade:
- In a bowl, whisk together olive oil, fresh lemon juice, minced garlic, dried thyme, dried rosemary, dried oregano, salt, and black pepper.

Coat Vegetables:
- Place the chopped vegetables in a large bowl. Pour the lemon herb marinade over the vegetables and toss until they are evenly coated.

Roast Vegetables:
- Spread the coated vegetables in a single layer on a baking sheet lined with parchment paper or a lightly greased baking dish.

Bake:
- Roast the vegetables in the preheated oven for 25-30 minutes or until they are tender and golden brown, stirring halfway through for even cooking.

Zest Lemon:
- While the vegetables are roasting, zest one lemon to add a burst of fresh flavor.

Garnish and Serve:
- Once the vegetables are done, remove them from the oven. Sprinkle the lemon zest over the roasted vegetables and toss gently. Garnish with fresh parsley if desired.

Serve:
- Serve the lemon herb roasted vegetables hot as a flavorful and colorful side dish.

This dish not only enhances the natural flavors of the vegetables but also adds a bright and citrusy twist with the combination of lemon and herbs. It's a versatile recipe that pairs well with various main dishes. Enjoy these lemon herb roasted vegetables as a healthy and delicious addition to your meals!

Miso Glazed Cod

Ingredients:

- 4 cod fillets (about 6 ounces each)
- 3 tablespoons white miso paste
- 2 tablespoons mirin (Japanese sweet rice wine)
- 1 tablespoon soy sauce
- 1 tablespoon rice vinegar
- 1 tablespoon honey or maple syrup
- 1 teaspoon sesame oil
- 1 teaspoon fresh ginger, grated
- 2 green onions, thinly sliced (for garnish)
- Sesame seeds (for garnish)

Instructions:

Preheat Oven:
- Preheat your oven to 400°F (200°C).

Prepare Miso Glaze:
- In a bowl, whisk together white miso paste, mirin, soy sauce, rice vinegar, honey or maple syrup, sesame oil, and grated ginger until well combined.

Marinate Cod:
- Place the cod fillets in a shallow dish or a resealable plastic bag. Pour half of the miso glaze over the cod fillets, making sure they are well-coated. Reserve the remaining glaze for later.

Marinate Time:
- Allow the cod to marinate for at least 15-20 minutes to let the flavors infuse.

Bake:
- Transfer the marinated cod fillets to a baking dish lined with parchment paper or lightly greased. Bake in the preheated oven for 12-15 minutes or until the cod is cooked through and flakes easily with a fork.

Glaze Cod:
- In the last few minutes of baking, brush the reserved miso glaze over the cod fillets for a glossy finish.

Garnish:
- Once the cod is done, remove it from the oven and garnish with thinly sliced green onions and sesame seeds.

Serve:
- Serve the miso-glazed cod hot over a bed of steamed rice or alongside your favorite vegetables.

This miso-glazed cod recipe offers a perfect balance of savory, sweet, and umami flavors. The miso glaze not only imparts richness to the cod but also creates a beautiful caramelized crust during baking. Enjoy this elegant and delicious dish for a delightful dining experience!

Stuffed Portobello Mushrooms

Ingredients:

- 4 large Portobello mushrooms, stems removed and cleaned
- 2 tablespoons olive oil
- 1 small onion, finely chopped
- 2 cloves garlic, minced
- 1 cup spinach, chopped
- 1/2 cup breadcrumbs
- 1/4 cup grated Parmesan cheese
- 1/4 cup chopped fresh herbs (such as parsley, thyme, or rosemary)
- Salt and black pepper to taste
- 1/2 cup shredded mozzarella or your favorite cheese (optional)
- Cherry tomatoes for garnish (optional)

Instructions:

Preheat Oven:
- Preheat your oven to 375°F (190°C).

Prepare Portobello Mushrooms:
- Remove the stems from the Portobello mushrooms and clean them gently with a damp cloth or paper towel.

Sauté Onion and Garlic:
- In a skillet, heat olive oil over medium heat. Add finely chopped onion and cook until softened. Add minced garlic and sauté for an additional 1-2 minutes.

Add Spinach:
- Add chopped spinach to the skillet and cook until wilted. Remove the skillet from heat.

Prepare Filling:
- In a bowl, combine the sautéed onion, garlic, and spinach mixture with breadcrumbs, grated Parmesan cheese, chopped fresh herbs, salt, and black pepper. Mix well to create the stuffing.

Stuff Mushrooms:
- Place the cleaned Portobello mushrooms on a baking sheet. Spoon the stuffing mixture into each mushroom cap, pressing it down gently.

Add Cheese (Optional):

- If desired, sprinkle shredded mozzarella or your favorite cheese over the stuffed mushrooms.

Bake:
- Bake in the preheated oven for 15-20 minutes or until the mushrooms are tender, and the cheese (if added) is melted and bubbly.

Garnish (Optional):
- Garnish the stuffed Portobello mushrooms with cherry tomatoes or additional herbs.

Serve:
- Serve the stuffed Portobello mushrooms hot as an appetizer, side dish, or main course.

Feel free to customize the stuffing with your favorite ingredients, such as sun-dried tomatoes, chopped nuts, or crumbled feta cheese. Stuffed Portobello mushrooms are a versatile dish that allows for creativity and variation based on your preferences. Enjoy these flavorful and hearty stuffed mushrooms!

Cucumber Avocado Soup

Ingredients:

- 2 large cucumbers, peeled and diced
- 2 ripe avocados, peeled and pitted
- 1 cup plain Greek yogurt
- 1/4 cup fresh mint leaves
- 1/4 cup fresh cilantro leaves
- 1 clove garlic, minced
- 2 tablespoons fresh lime or lemon juice
- 2 cups vegetable or chicken broth, chilled
- Salt and black pepper to taste
- Ice cubes (optional, for serving)
- Extra mint and cilantro for garnish

Instructions:

Prepare Ingredients:
- Peel and dice the cucumbers. Peel and pit the avocados.

Blend Ingredients:
- In a blender, combine diced cucumbers, avocados, Greek yogurt, mint leaves, cilantro leaves, minced garlic, lime or lemon juice, and chilled vegetable or chicken broth.

Blend Until Smooth:
- Blend the ingredients until smooth and creamy. If the soup is too thick, you can add more chilled broth to reach your desired consistency.

Season:
- Season the soup with salt and black pepper to taste. Adjust the seasoning as needed.

Chill:
- Refrigerate the cucumber avocado soup for at least 1-2 hours to allow the flavors to meld and the soup to become nicely chilled.

Serve:
- Ladle the chilled soup into bowls. If desired, add ice cubes to each serving bowl for an extra refreshing touch.

Garnish:
- Garnish the soup with additional mint and cilantro leaves.

Enjoy:
- Serve the cucumber avocado soup as a light and refreshing appetizer or a cool summer meal.

This cucumber avocado soup is not only delicious but also packed with healthy fats and refreshing flavors. The combination of cucumber and avocado creates a creamy texture, while the herbs and lime juice add a burst of freshness. Enjoy this cold soup on a warm day for a satisfying and nourishing experience!

Cilantro Lime Rice with Black Beans

Ingredients:

- 1 cup long-grain white rice
- 2 cups water or vegetable broth
- 1 can (15 ounces) black beans, drained and rinsed
- 1/4 cup fresh cilantro, chopped
- 1-2 limes, juiced
- 2 tablespoons olive oil
- 2 cloves garlic, minced
- Salt and black pepper to taste
- Optional toppings: diced tomatoes, diced avocado, sliced green onions

Instructions:

Cook Rice:
- Rinse the rice under cold water until the water runs clear. In a saucepan, combine the rice and water or vegetable broth. Bring to a boil, then reduce the heat to low, cover, and simmer for 15-20 minutes or until the rice is tender and the liquid is absorbed.

Fluff Rice:
- Once the rice is cooked, fluff it with a fork to separate the grains.

Prepare Black Beans:
- In a separate pan, heat the olive oil over medium heat. Add minced garlic and sauté for about 1 minute until fragrant. Add the black beans and cook for an additional 3-5 minutes until heated through.

Combine Rice and Beans:
- Add the cooked black beans to the fluffed rice. Mix gently to combine.

Add Cilantro and Lime:
- Add chopped cilantro to the rice and beans. Squeeze the juice of one or two limes over the mixture, depending on your taste preference.

Season:
- Season the cilantro lime rice with salt and black pepper to taste. Adjust the seasoning as needed.

Toss and Serve:
- Toss the ingredients together until well combined. Serve the cilantro lime rice with black beans hot.

Optional Toppings:
- If desired, top the cilantro lime rice with diced tomatoes, diced avocado, sliced green onions, or your favorite toppings.

Enjoy:
- Enjoy this flavorful and vibrant cilantro lime rice with black beans as a side dish or a wholesome vegetarian main course.

This dish is not only delicious but also versatile. You can customize it with your favorite toppings or add grilled vegetables for extra flavor and nutrition. It's a perfect accompaniment to Mexican or Tex-Mex-inspired meals or enjoyed on its own for a tasty and satisfying dish!

Baked Chicken with Mustard and Herbs

Ingredients:

- 4 boneless, skinless chicken breasts
- 2 tablespoons Dijon mustard
- 2 tablespoons whole-grain mustard
- 2 tablespoons olive oil
- 2 cloves garlic, minced
- 1 tablespoon fresh thyme leaves (or 1 teaspoon dried thyme)
- 1 tablespoon fresh rosemary, chopped (or 1 teaspoon dried rosemary)
- Salt and black pepper to taste
- Lemon wedges for serving

Instructions:

Preheat Oven:
- Preheat your oven to 400°F (200°C).

Prepare Chicken:
- Pat the chicken breasts dry with paper towels. Season them with salt and black pepper on both sides.

Mix Mustard Marinade:
- In a small bowl, whisk together Dijon mustard, whole-grain mustard, olive oil, minced garlic, fresh thyme leaves, and chopped rosemary.

Coat Chicken:
- Place the chicken breasts in a baking dish. Brush the mustard and herb marinade over each chicken breast, making sure they are well-coated.

Bake:
- Bake in the preheated oven for approximately 25-30 minutes or until the chicken is cooked through and no longer pink in the center. The internal temperature should reach 165°F (74°C).

Broil (Optional):
- If you want to achieve a golden brown crust on top, you can broil the chicken for an additional 2-3 minutes at the end of the cooking time.

Serve:
- Remove the baked chicken from the oven and let it rest for a few minutes. Serve the chicken with lemon wedges on the side.

Enjoy:

- Enjoy this baked chicken with mustard and herbs as a tasty and fuss-free main course.

Feel free to customize the herbs and adjust the quantities based on your preferences. This recipe provides a delicious combination of tangy mustard and aromatic herbs, creating a flavorful and juicy baked chicken. Pair it with your favorite side dishes for a complete and satisfying meal!

Mango Basil Chicken Lettuce Wraps

Ingredients:

For the Chicken:

- 1 pound boneless, skinless chicken breasts, cooked and shredded
- 2 tablespoons soy sauce
- 1 tablespoon sesame oil
- 1 tablespoon honey or maple syrup
- 1 teaspoon fresh ginger, grated
- 2 cloves garlic, minced
- 1 tablespoon rice vinegar
- Salt and pepper to taste

For the Mango Basil Salsa:

- 1 large ripe mango, diced
- 1/4 cup fresh basil, chopped
- 1/4 cup red onion, finely diced
- 1 tablespoon lime juice
- Salt and pepper to taste

For Assembling Lettuce Wraps:

- Large lettuce leaves (such as butter lettuce or iceberg)
- Cooked and shredded chicken
- Mango basil salsa
- Optional toppings: chopped peanuts, chopped cilantro, extra lime wedges

Instructions:

Prepare Chicken:
- Cook the chicken breasts and shred them. In a bowl, mix the shredded chicken with soy sauce, sesame oil, honey or maple syrup, grated ginger, minced garlic, rice vinegar, salt, and pepper. Toss until the chicken is well-coated with the marinade.

Prepare Mango Basil Salsa:

- In another bowl, combine diced mango, chopped basil, finely diced red onion, lime juice, salt, and pepper. Mix well to create the mango basil salsa.

Assemble Lettuce Wraps:
- Take a large lettuce leaf and spoon some of the shredded chicken onto it.

Add Mango Basil Salsa:
- Top the chicken with a generous spoonful of mango basil salsa.

Optional Toppings:
- Optionally, sprinkle chopped peanuts and cilantro over the top for added crunch and flavor.

Serve:
- Serve the mango basil chicken lettuce wraps immediately, with extra lime wedges on the side.

Enjoy:
- Enjoy these refreshing and vibrant lettuce wraps as a light and delicious meal!

These mango basil chicken lettuce wraps are not only packed with flavor but also provide a delightful combination of sweet and savory elements. They make for a perfect appetizer, lunch, or dinner option, especially during warmer weather when you're craving something fresh and satisfying.

Spaghetti Squash Primavera

Ingredients:

- 1 medium-sized spaghetti squash
- 2 tablespoons olive oil
- 1 small red onion, thinly sliced
- 2 cloves garlic, minced
- 1 bell pepper, thinly sliced
- 1 zucchini, thinly sliced
- 1 carrot, julienned or thinly sliced
- 1 cup cherry tomatoes, halved
- 1/2 cup broccoli florets
- 1/2 cup snap peas, trimmed
- Salt and black pepper to taste
- 1/2 teaspoon dried oregano
- 1/2 teaspoon dried basil
- Grated Parmesan cheese for serving (optional)
- Fresh basil or parsley for garnish

Instructions:

Preheat Oven:
- Preheat your oven to 400°F (200°C).

Prepare Spaghetti Squash:
- Cut the spaghetti squash in half lengthwise. Scoop out the seeds and pulp. Place the squash halves on a baking sheet, cut side up.

Bake Spaghetti Squash:
- Bake the spaghetti squash in the preheated oven for about 40-45 minutes or until the flesh is tender. Use a fork to scrape the strands of spaghetti-like flesh from the squash.

Sauté Vegetables:
- While the spaghetti squash is baking, heat olive oil in a large skillet over medium heat. Add sliced red onion and minced garlic. Sauté for 2-3 minutes until the onion is softened.

Add Vegetables:
- Add sliced bell pepper, zucchini, julienned carrot, cherry tomatoes, broccoli florets, and snap peas to the skillet. Sauté for an additional 5-7 minutes until the vegetables are tender-crisp.

Season:
- Season the vegetables with salt, black pepper, dried oregano, and dried basil. Adjust the seasoning to your taste.

Combine with Spaghetti Squash:
- Add the scraped spaghetti squash strands to the skillet with the sautéed vegetables. Toss everything together until well combined.

Serve:
- Divide the spaghetti squash primavera among plates. If desired, sprinkle grated Parmesan cheese on top and garnish with fresh basil or parsley.

Enjoy:
- Enjoy this spaghetti squash primavera as a light and nutritious alternative to traditional pasta dishes.

This dish is not only delicious and satisfying but also low in calories and packed with nutrients. It's a great way to enjoy a classic primavera with the added benefit of spaghetti squash replacing traditional pasta.

Cumin-Spiced Lentils

Ingredients:

- 1 cup dried lentils (green or brown), rinsed and drained
- 3 cups water or vegetable broth
- 1 tablespoon olive oil
- 1 onion, finely chopped
- 2 cloves garlic, minced
- 1 teaspoon ground cumin
- 1/2 teaspoon ground coriander
- 1/2 teaspoon smoked paprika
- 1/4 teaspoon cayenne pepper (adjust to taste)
- Salt and black pepper to taste
- 1 can (14 ounces) diced tomatoes, undrained
- Fresh cilantro for garnish (optional)
- Lemon wedges for serving

Instructions:

Cook Lentils:
- In a medium saucepan, combine the lentils and water or vegetable broth. Bring to a boil, then reduce the heat to low, cover, and simmer for 20-25 minutes or until the lentils are tender but not mushy. Drain any excess liquid.

Sauté Onion and Garlic:
- In a large skillet, heat olive oil over medium heat. Add finely chopped onion and sauté until softened. Add minced garlic and cook for an additional 1-2 minutes.

Add Spices:
- Add ground cumin, ground coriander, smoked paprika, cayenne pepper, salt, and black pepper to the skillet. Stir well to coat the onions and garlic with the spices.

Combine with Lentils:
- Add the cooked lentils to the skillet with the spiced onion mixture. Stir to combine.

Add Tomatoes:

- Pour the diced tomatoes with their juices into the skillet. Stir well and let the mixture simmer for an additional 5-7 minutes, allowing the flavors to meld.

Adjust Seasoning:
- Taste the cumin-spiced lentils and adjust the seasoning as needed. Add more salt, pepper, or cayenne pepper according to your preference.

Serve:
- Garnish with fresh cilantro if desired and serve the cumin-spiced lentils hot. Optionally, serve with lemon wedges on the side.

Enjoy:
- Enjoy these flavorful cumin-spiced lentils as a side dish, over rice, or as a vegetarian main course.

This dish is rich in protein and fiber, making it a nutritious and satisfying addition to your meals. The combination of cumin, coriander, and smoked paprika adds a warm and aromatic flavor to the lentils. Serve them with a squeeze of fresh lemon juice for a burst of citrusy freshness.

Herb-Roasted Turkey BreastHerb-Roasted Turkey Breast

Ingredients:

- 1 whole bone-in turkey breast (about 5-6 pounds)
- 2 tablespoons olive oil
- 2 teaspoons dried thyme
- 2 teaspoons dried rosemary
- 2 teaspoons dried sage
- 1 teaspoon dried oregano
- 1 teaspoon garlic powder
- Salt and black pepper to taste
- 1 cup chicken or turkey broth (for basting)
- Optional: 1 onion and 2 carrots, roughly chopped (for roasting)

Instructions:

Preheat Oven:
- Preheat your oven to 325°F (163°C).

Prepare Turkey Breast:
- Rinse the turkey breast under cold water and pat it dry with paper towels. Place the turkey breast on a roasting rack set inside a roasting pan.

Herb Rub:
- In a small bowl, mix together olive oil, dried thyme, dried rosemary, dried sage, dried oregano, garlic powder, salt, and black pepper to form a herb rub.

Rub the Turkey:
- Rub the herb mixture all over the surface of the turkey breast, making sure to coat it evenly.

Optional Vegetables:
- If desired, scatter roughly chopped onion and carrots in the roasting pan around the turkey breast. These vegetables can add flavor to the drippings and serve as a bed for the turkey.

Roast:
- Place the turkey breast in the preheated oven. Roast for about 2 to 2.5 hours, basting the turkey with chicken or turkey broth every 30 minutes. If the skin starts to brown too quickly, cover the turkey loosely with aluminum foil.

Check Temperature:
- Check the internal temperature of the turkey breast using a meat thermometer. The turkey is done when the internal temperature reaches 165°F (74°C) in the thickest part of the breast.

Rest:
- Once the turkey is done, remove it from the oven and let it rest for about 15 minutes before carving. This allows the juices to redistribute, keeping the meat moist.

Carve:
- Carve the herb-roasted turkey breast into slices and serve.

Enjoy:
- Enjoy the herb-roasted turkey breast with your favorite sides and gravy.

This herb-roasted turkey breast is seasoned with a blend of aromatic herbs, creating a delicious and savory flavor. It's a wonderful option for a smaller gathering or when you're craving turkey outside of the holiday season.

Ratatouille

Ingredients:

- 1 large eggplant, diced
- 2 medium zucchini, diced
- 1 large red bell pepper, diced
- 1 large yellow bell pepper, diced
- 1 large onion, finely chopped
- 3 cloves garlic, minced
- 3 large tomatoes, diced
- 2 tablespoons tomato paste
- 1 teaspoon dried thyme
- 1 teaspoon dried rosemary
- 1 teaspoon dried oregano
- Salt and black pepper to taste
- 1/4 cup fresh basil, chopped
- 1/4 cup fresh parsley, chopped
- Olive oil for cooking

Instructions:

Prepare Vegetables:
- Dice the eggplant, zucchini, red bell pepper, yellow bell pepper, and tomatoes into uniform-sized pieces.

Sauté Onion and Garlic:
- In a large, deep skillet or a Dutch oven, heat olive oil over medium heat. Add the finely chopped onion and sauté until softened, about 3-4 minutes. Add minced garlic and cook for an additional 1-2 minutes until fragrant.

Add Eggplant and Zucchini:
- Add the diced eggplant and zucchini to the skillet. Cook for about 5-7 minutes until they begin to soften.

Add Bell Peppers:
- Stir in the diced red and yellow bell peppers and continue cooking for an additional 5 minutes.

Add Tomatoes and Tomato Paste:
- Add the diced tomatoes and tomato paste to the skillet. Stir well to combine.

Season:
- Season the mixture with dried thyme, dried rosemary, dried oregano, salt, and black pepper. Stir to distribute the herbs evenly.

Simmer:
- Reduce the heat to low, cover the skillet, and let the ratatouille simmer for about 20-25 minutes, stirring occasionally, until all the vegetables are tender.

Finish with Fresh Herbs:
- Stir in the chopped fresh basil and parsley. Adjust the seasoning if needed.

Serve:
- Serve the ratatouille warm as a side dish or a vegetarian main course.

Enjoy:
- Enjoy this classic ratatouille with crusty bread, over rice, or on its own.

Ratatouille is a versatile dish that can be enjoyed on its own or as a side to various proteins. It's a celebration of the vibrant flavors of seasonal vegetables, making it a delightful and healthy option for any meal.

Turkey and Vegetable Kabobs

Ingredients:

For the Marinade:

- 1/4 cup olive oil
- 2 tablespoons soy sauce
- 2 tablespoons honey
- 2 cloves garlic, minced
- 1 teaspoon Dijon mustard
- 1 teaspoon dried oregano
- 1 teaspoon dried thyme
- Salt and black pepper to taste

For the Kabobs:

- 1.5 pounds turkey breast, cut into 1-inch cubes
- 1 red bell pepper, cut into chunks
- 1 yellow bell pepper, cut into chunks
- 1 red onion, cut into chunks
- 1 zucchini, sliced into rounds
- Cherry tomatoes
- Wooden or metal skewers (if using wooden skewers, soak them in water for 30 minutes before using)

Instructions:

Prepare Marinade:
- In a bowl, whisk together olive oil, soy sauce, honey, minced garlic, Dijon mustard, dried oregano, dried thyme, salt, and black pepper to create the marinade.

Marinate Turkey:
- Place the turkey cubes in a resealable plastic bag or a shallow dish. Pour half of the marinade over the turkey, making sure it's well-coated. Reserve the other half for basting during grilling. Marinate the turkey in the refrigerator for at least 30 minutes or up to 4 hours.

Prepare Vegetables:

- While the turkey is marinating, prepare the vegetables by cutting the bell peppers, red onion, zucchini, and any other desired vegetables into chunks or slices.

Assemble Kabobs:
- Preheat the grill to medium-high heat. Thread the marinated turkey cubes and prepared vegetables onto the skewers, alternating between turkey and vegetables.

Grill Kabobs:
- Place the kabobs on the preheated grill and cook for about 10-12 minutes, turning occasionally, until the turkey is cooked through and the vegetables are tender.

Baste with Marinade:
- During the last few minutes of grilling, baste the kabobs with the reserved marinade for added flavor.

Serve:
- Remove the turkey and vegetable kabobs from the grill. Serve them hot, and optionally, garnish with fresh herbs.

Enjoy:
- Enjoy these flavorful and juicy turkey and vegetable kabobs as a wholesome and satisfying meal.

These kabobs are a fantastic way to enjoy a mix of lean protein and colorful vegetables. They are great for summer grilling or any time you want a tasty and healthy dish. Serve them with a side of rice, quinoa, or a fresh salad for a complete and balanced meal.

Stuffed Acorn Squash

Ingredients:

- 2 acorn squash, halved and seeds removed
- 1 cup quinoa, rinsed
- 2 cups vegetable broth or water
- 1 tablespoon olive oil
- 1 onion, finely chopped
- 2 cloves garlic, minced
- 1 carrot, diced
- 1 celery stalk, diced
- 1 bell pepper, diced (any color)
- 1 zucchini, diced
- 1 teaspoon dried thyme
- 1 teaspoon dried sage
- Salt and black pepper to taste
- 1/2 cup dried cranberries or raisins (optional)
- 1/2 cup chopped nuts (walnuts, pecans, or almonds)
- Fresh parsley or cilantro for garnish

Instructions:

Preheat Oven:
- Preheat your oven to 400°F (200°C).

Roast Acorn Squash:
- Place the halved acorn squash on a baking sheet, cut side up. Brush the cut sides with olive oil and sprinkle with salt and pepper. Roast in the preheated oven for about 30-40 minutes or until the squash is tender.

Cook Quinoa:
- While the squash is roasting, rinse the quinoa under cold water. In a saucepan, combine the quinoa and vegetable broth or water. Bring to a boil, then reduce heat, cover, and simmer for 15-20 minutes or until the quinoa is cooked and liquid is absorbed.

Sauté Vegetables:
- In a large skillet, heat olive oil over medium heat. Add chopped onion, minced garlic, diced carrot, diced celery, diced bell pepper, and diced zucchini. Sauté for 8-10 minutes until the vegetables are softened.

Season:

- Season the sautéed vegetables with dried thyme, dried sage, salt, and black pepper. Stir in the cooked quinoa, dried cranberries or raisins (if using), and chopped nuts.

Stuff Acorn Squash:
- Once the acorn squash halves are tender, stuff them with the quinoa and vegetable mixture.

Bake:
- Return the stuffed acorn squash to the oven and bake for an additional 10-15 minutes until everything is heated through.

Garnish:
- Garnish the stuffed acorn squash with fresh parsley or cilantro before serving.

Serve:
- Serve the stuffed acorn squash as a wholesome and flavorful main course.

This stuffed acorn squash recipe provides a delightful combination of sweet and savory flavors, along with a variety of textures. Feel free to customize the filling with your favorite herbs, spices, or additional vegetables for a personal touch. Enjoy this comforting and nutritious dish!

Garlic Lemon Shrimp with Quinoa

Ingredients:

- 1 cup quinoa, rinsed
- 2 cups chicken or vegetable broth
- 1 pound large shrimp, peeled and deveined
- 4 tablespoons olive oil, divided
- 4 cloves garlic, minced
- Zest of 1 lemon
- Juice of 1 lemon
- 1 teaspoon dried oregano
- Salt and black pepper to taste
- Fresh parsley, chopped, for garnish
- Lemon wedges for serving

Instructions:

Cook Quinoa:
- In a medium saucepan, combine quinoa and chicken or vegetable broth. Bring to a boil, then reduce the heat to low, cover, and simmer for 15-20 minutes or until the quinoa is cooked and the liquid is absorbed.

Prepare Shrimp:
- In a large bowl, toss the shrimp with minced garlic, lemon zest, lemon juice, dried oregano, salt, and black pepper. Let it marinate for about 10 minutes.

Cook Shrimp:
- In a large skillet, heat 2 tablespoons of olive oil over medium-high heat. Add the marinated shrimp and cook for 2-3 minutes on each side or until they are opaque and cooked through. Remove the shrimp from the skillet and set aside.

Sauté Quinoa:
- In the same skillet, add the remaining 2 tablespoons of olive oil. Add the cooked quinoa and sauté for 2-3 minutes, allowing it to absorb the flavors.

Combine Shrimp and Quinoa:
- Add the cooked shrimp back to the skillet with the quinoa. Toss everything together until well combined and heated through.

Garnish:
- Garnish the garlic lemon shrimp with quinoa with chopped fresh parsley.

Serve:
- Serve the dish hot, with lemon wedges on the side for an extra burst of citrus flavor.

Enjoy:
- Enjoy this garlic lemon shrimp with quinoa as a light and flavorful meal.

This dish is not only delicious but also a balanced and nutritious option. The combination of garlic, lemon, and herbs adds a zesty and aromatic touch to the succulent shrimp, and the quinoa provides a protein-packed and wholesome base. It's a quick and easy recipe that's perfect for a weeknight dinner.

Cabbage and Carrot Slaw

Ingredients:

For the Slaw:

- 4 cups shredded green cabbage (about 1 small cabbage)
- 1 cup grated carrots (about 2 medium carrots)
- 1/2 cup chopped fresh parsley or cilantro

For the Dressing:

- 1/4 cup mayonnaise
- 2 tablespoons plain Greek yogurt or sour cream
- 2 tablespoons apple cider vinegar
- 1 tablespoon Dijon mustard
- 1 tablespoon honey or maple syrup
- Salt and black pepper to taste

Instructions:

Prepare Vegetables:
- Shred the green cabbage and grate the carrots. If you prefer a finer texture, you can use a food processor with a shredding attachment.

Chop Herbs:
- Chop the fresh parsley or cilantro.

Make Dressing:
- In a small bowl, whisk together mayonnaise, Greek yogurt or sour cream, apple cider vinegar, Dijon mustard, honey or maple syrup, salt, and black pepper. Adjust the sweetness and acidity to your taste.

Combine Slaw Ingredients:
- In a large mixing bowl, combine the shredded cabbage, grated carrots, and chopped herbs.

Dress the Slaw:
- Pour the dressing over the cabbage and carrot mixture. Toss everything together until the vegetables are evenly coated with the dressing.

Chill (Optional):
- For optimal flavor, you can cover the slaw and refrigerate it for at least 30 minutes before serving. This allows the flavors to meld.

Serve:
- Serve the cabbage and carrot slaw as a refreshing side dish.

Enjoy:
- Enjoy this crisp and colorful slaw alongside grilled meats, sandwiches, tacos, or as a topping for fish tacos.

Feel free to customize this slaw recipe by adding other ingredients like thinly sliced red onion, bell peppers, or even a handful of raisins for sweetness. It's a versatile dish that can be adapted to your preferences and complements a wide range of dishes.

Mushroom and Spinach Stuffed Portobello Mushrooms

Ingredients:

- 4 large portobello mushrooms, stems removed
- 2 tablespoons olive oil
- 1 onion, finely chopped
- 2 cloves garlic, minced
- 8 ounces (about 225g) baby spinach, chopped
- 8 ounces (about 225g) mushrooms, finely chopped (you can use cremini or white mushrooms)
- 1/2 cup breadcrumbs
- 1/2 cup grated Parmesan cheese
- Salt and black pepper to taste
- 1 teaspoon dried thyme
- 1/2 cup shredded mozzarella cheese (optional)
- Fresh parsley, chopped, for garnish

Instructions:

Preheat Oven:
- Preheat your oven to 375°F (190°C).

Prepare Portobello Mushrooms:
- Clean the portobello mushrooms and remove the stems. Place them on a baking sheet lined with parchment paper or aluminum foil.

Sauté Onion and Garlic:
- In a large skillet, heat olive oil over medium heat. Add finely chopped onion and sauté until softened. Add minced garlic and cook for an additional 1-2 minutes.

Add Spinach and Mushrooms:
- Add chopped baby spinach and mushrooms to the skillet. Cook until the spinach is wilted, and the mushrooms release their moisture.

Combine Ingredients:
- Stir in breadcrumbs, grated Parmesan cheese, salt, black pepper, and dried thyme. Cook for an additional 2-3 minutes, allowing the mixture to come together.

Stuff Portobello Mushrooms:

- Spoon the spinach and mushroom mixture into the hollowed-out portobello mushrooms.

Optional Cheese Topping:
- If desired, sprinkle shredded mozzarella cheese on top of each stuffed mushroom for added richness.

Bake:
- Bake in the preheated oven for 15-20 minutes or until the mushrooms are tender and the filling is golden brown.

Garnish:
- Garnish with fresh chopped parsley before serving.

Serve:
- Serve the mushroom and spinach stuffed portobello mushrooms hot.

These stuffed portobello mushrooms make a fantastic appetizer or a light main course. The combination of earthy mushrooms, vibrant spinach, and savory Parmesan creates a satisfying and flavorful dish. Enjoy them on their own or pair them with a side salad for a complete meal.

Baked Cod with Mango Salsa

Baked Cod:

Ingredients:

- 4 cod fillets (about 6 ounces each)
- 2 tablespoons olive oil
- 1 teaspoon paprika
- 1 teaspoon garlic powder
- 1 teaspoon onion powder
- Salt and black pepper to taste
- Fresh lemon wedges for serving

Instructions:

Preheat Oven:
- Preheat your oven to 400°F (200°C).

Prepare Cod:
- Pat the cod fillets dry with paper towels. Place them on a baking sheet lined with parchment paper.

Season Cod:
- In a small bowl, mix together olive oil, paprika, garlic powder, onion powder, salt, and black pepper. Brush the cod fillets with the seasoned olive oil mixture.

Bake:
- Bake the cod in the preheated oven for 12-15 minutes or until the fish is opaque and flakes easily with a fork.

Serve:
- Remove the baked cod from the oven and squeeze fresh lemon juice over the fillets. Serve hot.

Mango Salsa:

Ingredients:

- 1 ripe mango, peeled and diced
- 1/2 red onion, finely chopped
- 1 red bell pepper, diced
- 1/4 cup fresh cilantro, chopped
- Juice of 1 lime
- Salt and black pepper to taste

Instructions:

- Prepare Mango Salsa:
    - In a bowl, combine diced mango, chopped red onion, diced red bell pepper, fresh cilantro, lime juice, salt, and black pepper. Mix well.
- Chill (Optional):
    - For enhanced flavors, you can cover the salsa and refrigerate it for about 30 minutes before serving.

Serving:

- Place the baked cod fillets on individual plates.
- Top each cod fillet with a generous spoonful of mango salsa.
- Garnish with extra cilantro if desired.
- Serve immediately and enjoy!

This dish is a perfect balance of light and vibrant flavors. The tender and flaky cod pairs beautifully with the sweet and tangy mango salsa, creating a delicious and healthy meal. Serve it with your favorite side dishes or a bed of quinoa or rice for a complete dining experience.

Sweet Potato and Kale Frittata

Ingredients:

- 1 medium sweet potato, peeled and thinly sliced
- 2 cups kale, stems removed and chopped
- 1 small onion, finely chopped
- 8 large eggs
- 1/4 cup milk (dairy or plant-based)
- Salt and black pepper to taste
- 1 teaspoon olive oil
- 1/2 cup shredded cheese (cheddar, feta, or goat cheese work well)
- Fresh herbs (such as parsley or chives) for garnish (optional)

Instructions:

Preheat Oven:
- Preheat your oven to 375°F (190°C).

Cook Sweet Potatoes:
- In a skillet over medium heat, add olive oil. Cook the thinly sliced sweet potatoes until they are tender, about 5-7 minutes. Remove them from the skillet and set aside.

Sauté Kale and Onion:
- In the same skillet, add chopped kale and finely chopped onion. Sauté until the kale is wilted and the onion is softened.

Whisk Eggs:
- In a bowl, whisk together eggs, milk, salt, and black pepper.

Assemble Frittata:
- Grease a baking dish or oven-safe skillet. Arrange the cooked sweet potato slices on the bottom. Spread the sautéed kale and onion over the sweet potatoes. Pour the whisked eggs over the vegetables.

Add Cheese:
- Sprinkle shredded cheese evenly over the frittata.

Bake:
- Transfer the baking dish or skillet to the preheated oven. Bake for 20-25 minutes or until the eggs are set and the top is golden brown.

Garnish:
- If desired, garnish the frittata with fresh herbs.

Serve:
- Allow the frittata to cool slightly before slicing. Serve it warm.

Optional Additions:

- You can customize the frittata by adding diced bell peppers, cherry tomatoes, or mushrooms.
- Experiment with different herbs and spices like thyme, rosemary, or smoked paprika for added flavor.

This sweet potato and kale frittata is not only delicious but also packed with nutrients. It's a versatile dish that allows you to get creative with the ingredients based on your preferences. Serve it with a side salad for a complete and satisfying meal.

Tomato and Basil Stuffed Chicken Breast

Ingredients:

- 4 boneless, skinless chicken breasts
- Salt and black pepper to taste
- 1 teaspoon dried oregano
- 1 teaspoon garlic powder
- 4 ounces mozzarella cheese, sliced
- 2 large tomatoes, sliced
- Fresh basil leaves
- Olive oil for drizzling
- Balsamic glaze for serving (optional)

Instructions:

Preheat Oven:
- Preheat your oven to 400°F (200°C).

Prepare Chicken Breasts:
- Lay each chicken breast on a cutting board. Using a sharp knife, make a horizontal slit along the side of each chicken breast to create a pocket. Be careful not to cut all the way through.

Season Chicken:
- Season the inside and outside of each chicken breast with salt, black pepper, dried oregano, and garlic powder.

Stuff with Tomatoes, Basil, and Cheese:
- Stuff each chicken breast with slices of mozzarella cheese, tomato, and fresh basil leaves. Try to distribute them evenly inside the pocket.

Secure with Toothpicks:
- If needed, secure the open side of each chicken breast with toothpicks to help hold the stuffing in place during cooking.

Drizzle with Olive Oil:
- Place the stuffed chicken breasts on a baking sheet. Drizzle olive oil over the top of each chicken breast.

Bake:
- Bake in the preheated oven for 25-30 minutes or until the chicken is cooked through and the internal temperature reaches 165°F (74°C).

Optional Broil:
- If you'd like to brown the top, you can briefly broil the chicken for 1-2 minutes, keeping a close eye to prevent burning.

Serve:
- Remove the toothpicks and serve the stuffed chicken breasts hot. Optionally, drizzle with balsamic glaze before serving.

Note:

- Make sure to let the chicken rest for a few minutes before slicing to allow the juices to redistribute.

This tomato and basil stuffed chicken breast is not only visually appealing but also bursting with fresh and savory flavors. It's a perfect dish for a special dinner or when you want to impress with a delicious and elegant meal.

Cauliflower and Chickpea Curry

Ingredients:

- 1 medium cauliflower, cut into florets
- 1 can (15 ounces) chickpeas, drained and rinsed
- 1 large onion, finely chopped
- 3 cloves garlic, minced
- 1 tablespoon fresh ginger, grated
- 1 can (14 ounces) diced tomatoes
- 1 can (14 ounces) coconut milk
- 2 tablespoons curry powder
- 1 teaspoon ground cumin
- 1 teaspoon ground coriander
- 1/2 teaspoon turmeric
- 1/4 teaspoon cayenne pepper (adjust to taste for spice level)
- Salt and black pepper to taste
- 2 tablespoons vegetable oil
- Fresh cilantro, chopped, for garnish
- Cooked rice or naan for serving

Instructions:

Sauté Aromatics:
- In a large skillet or pot, heat vegetable oil over medium heat. Add finely chopped onion and sauté until softened.

Add Garlic and Ginger:
- Add minced garlic and grated ginger to the skillet. Sauté for an additional 1-2 minutes until fragrant.

Spice Mix:
- Add curry powder, ground cumin, ground coriander, turmeric, cayenne pepper, salt, and black pepper to the skillet. Stir to coat the onions, garlic, and ginger with the spices.

Add Cauliflower and Chickpeas:
- Add cauliflower florets and drained chickpeas to the skillet. Stir to coat them with the spice mixture.

Tomatoes and Coconut Milk:
- Pour in diced tomatoes and coconut milk. Stir well, ensuring that the cauliflower and chickpeas are well coated in the curry sauce.

Simmer:

- Bring the curry to a simmer, then reduce the heat to low. Cover the skillet and let it simmer for about 15-20 minutes or until the cauliflower is tender.

Adjust Seasoning:
- Taste the curry and adjust the seasoning if needed. Add more salt, pepper, or spice according to your preferences.

Serve:
- Serve the cauliflower and chickpea curry over cooked rice or with naan. Garnish with chopped fresh cilantro.

Enjoy:
- Enjoy this flavorful and hearty cauliflower and chickpea curry as a delicious vegetarian meal.

This curry is not only delicious but also versatile. Feel free to customize it by adding other vegetables like spinach or peas. The combination of spices, coconut milk, and tomatoes creates a rich and aromatic sauce that complements the cauliflower and chickpeas perfectly.

Sautéed Spinach with Garlic

Ingredients:

- 1 pound fresh spinach, washed and stems removed
- 2 tablespoons olive oil
- 3-4 cloves garlic, minced
- Salt and black pepper to taste
- Red pepper flakes (optional, for a bit of heat)
- Lemon wedges for serving (optional)

Instructions:

Prepare Spinach:
- Wash the spinach thoroughly and remove any tough stems. If the leaves are large, you can also give them a rough chop.

Sauté Garlic:
- In a large skillet or pan, heat olive oil over medium heat. Add minced garlic and sauté for about 30 seconds to 1 minute until it becomes fragrant. Be careful not to let it brown too much.

Add Spinach:
- Add the washed and prepared spinach to the skillet. Toss gently to coat the spinach in the garlic-infused olive oil.

Sauté:
- Sauté the spinach for 2-3 minutes or until it wilts down. Keep tossing to ensure even cooking. The spinach will reduce in volume significantly.

Season:
- Season the sautéed spinach with salt, black pepper, and red pepper flakes (if using). Adjust the seasoning according to your taste.

Finish:
- Continue cooking for an additional 1-2 minutes until the spinach is fully wilted, but still vibrant green.

Serve:
- Transfer the sautéed spinach to a serving dish. Optionally, squeeze a bit of fresh lemon juice over the top before serving for a burst of brightness.

Enjoy:
- Serve the sautéed spinach with garlic as a side dish alongside your favorite main course.

This sautéed spinach recipe is a great way to enjoy the natural flavors of fresh spinach with the added kick of garlic. It's a versatile side dish that pairs well with a variety of proteins and can be easily customized with additional herbs or spices to suit your taste.

Baked Teriyaki Salmon

Ingredients:

- 4 salmon fillets
- 1/2 cup teriyaki sauce (store-bought or homemade)
- 2 tablespoons soy sauce
- 2 tablespoons honey or maple syrup
- 1 tablespoon rice vinegar
- 1 teaspoon sesame oil
- 2 cloves garlic, minced
- 1 teaspoon grated fresh ginger
- Sesame seeds and chopped green onions for garnish (optional)

Instructions:

Preheat Oven:
- Preheat your oven to 400°F (200°C).

Prepare Teriyaki Glaze:
- In a small saucepan, combine teriyaki sauce, soy sauce, honey or maple syrup, rice vinegar, sesame oil, minced garlic, and grated ginger. Bring to a simmer over medium heat and cook for 3-5 minutes, or until the sauce thickens slightly. Remove from heat and set aside.

Marinate Salmon:
- Place the salmon fillets in a dish or a zip-top bag. Pour half of the teriyaki glaze over the salmon, ensuring that each fillet is coated. Reserve the remaining glaze for later.

Marinate Time (Optional):
- Allow the salmon to marinate for at least 15-30 minutes. This step is optional but enhances the flavor.

Bake Salmon:
- Place the marinated salmon fillets on a baking sheet lined with parchment paper or lightly greased. Bake in the preheated oven for about 15-18 minutes, or until the salmon is cooked through and flakes easily with a fork.

Glaze Salmon:
- During the last 5 minutes of baking, brush the reserved teriyaki glaze over the salmon fillets. This adds extra flavor and creates a glossy finish.

Garnish:

- Once baked, garnish the teriyaki salmon with sesame seeds and chopped green onions, if desired.

Serve:
- Serve the baked teriyaki salmon hot with your favorite side dishes, such as rice or steamed vegetables.

Note:

- Be cautious not to overcook the salmon to keep it moist and tender. The cooking time may vary depending on the thickness of your salmon fillets.

This baked teriyaki salmon is a delightful dish with a perfect balance of sweet and savory flavors. It's a great choice for a quick and satisfying dinner.

Pineapple and Black Bean Quinoa Bowl

Ingredients:

For the Quinoa:

- 1 cup quinoa, rinsed
- 2 cups water or vegetable broth
- 1/2 teaspoon salt

For the Bowl:

- 1 can (15 ounces) black beans, drained and rinsed
- 1 cup pineapple chunks (fresh or canned)
- 1 red bell pepper, diced
- 1/4 cup red onion, finely chopped
- 1 avocado, sliced
- Fresh cilantro, chopped, for garnish
- Lime wedges for serving

For the Dressing:

- 3 tablespoons olive oil
- 2 tablespoons lime juice
- 1 tablespoon honey or maple syrup
- Salt and black pepper to taste

Instructions:

Cook Quinoa:
- In a medium saucepan, combine quinoa, water or vegetable broth, and salt. Bring to a boil, then reduce heat, cover, and simmer for 15-20 minutes or until the quinoa is cooked and liquid is absorbed. Fluff with a fork.

Prepare Dressing:
- In a small bowl, whisk together olive oil, lime juice, honey or maple syrup, salt, and black pepper. Set aside.

Assemble the Bowl:
- In serving bowls, arrange cooked quinoa, black beans, pineapple chunks, diced red bell pepper, chopped red onion, and sliced avocado.

Drizzle with Dressing:
- Drizzle the dressing over the ingredients in each bowl.

Garnish:

- Garnish the pineapple and black bean quinoa bowls with chopped fresh cilantro.

Serve:
- Serve the quinoa bowls with lime wedges on the side for an extra burst of citrus flavor.

Enjoy:
- Toss the ingredients together before eating and enjoy this vibrant and nutritious bowl.

Optional Additions:

- Add a handful of cherry tomatoes or cucumber slices for extra freshness.
- Top with crumbled feta or cotija cheese for a savory touch.
- Sprinkle with a pinch of chili powder or cayenne for a hint of spice.

This pineapple and black bean quinoa bowl is not only visually appealing but also a delightful mix of flavors and textures. It makes for a satisfying and healthy meal that you can easily customize based on your preferences.

www.ingramcontent.com/pod-product-compliance
Lightning Source LLC
LaVergne TN
LVHW061935070526
838199LV00060B/3838